Professional Learning in the Digital Age

The Educator's Guide to User-Generated Learning

Kristen Swanson

Eye On Education
6 Depot Way West, Suite 106
Larchmont, NY 10538
(914) 833–0551
(914) 833–0761 fax
www.eyeoneducation.com

Library of Congress Cataloging-in-Publication Data

Swanson, Kristen.
Professional learning in the digital age : the educator's guide to user-generated
learning / Kristen Swanson.
        p.   cm.
Includes bibliographical references.
ISBN 978-1-59667-228-4
1. Teachers-In-service training.
2. Educators—In-service training.
3. Professional learning communities.
4. Teaching—Computer network resources.
I. Title.
LB1731.S937 2012
370.71′1—dc23   2012029935

10 9 8 7 6 5 4 3 2 1

Sponsoring Editor: Robert Sickles
Production Editor: Lauren Beebe
Copyeditor: Laurie Lieb
Designer and Compositor: Matthew Williams, click! Publishing Services
Cover Designer: Armen Kojoyian

Also Available from Eye On Education

The School Leader's Guide to Social Media
Ronald Williamson & J. Howard Johnston

Step-by-Step Professional Development in Technology
Sarah T. Meltzer

Wikis for School Leaders:
Using Technology to Improve
Communication and Collaboration
Stephanie D. Sandifer

Organization Made Easy!
Tools for Today's Teachers
Frank Buck

The Learning Leader:
Reflecting, Modeling, and Sharing
Jacqueline E. Jacobs & Kevin L. O'Gorman

Communicate and Motivate:
The School Leader's Guide to Effective Communication
Shelly Arneson

Students Taking Charge:
Inside the Learner-Active, Technology-Infused Classroom
Nancy Sulla

Helping Students Motivate Themselves:
Practical Answers to Classroom Challenges
Larry Ferlazzo

What Great Teachers Do *Differently* (2nd Edition):
Seventeen Things That Matter Most
Todd Whitaker

To the original Edcamp Philly team:
Kevin, Kim, Dan, Marybeth, Rob, Mike,
Chrissi, Hadley, Ann, and Nicolae.

Thank you for giving me the courage to break
down the walls of professional learning.

Acknowledgments

This book was not written in isolation. I give thanks to the global network that has shaped my own learning and the ideas in this book. While there are too many people to thank individually, you know who you are!

I would also like to thank everyone at Eye On Education, especially Bob Sickles and Lauren Beebe. I am truly grateful to each of you for your unwavering belief in this book and me.

My gratitude also goes to Grant Wiggins and Denise Wilbur, the best bosses in the world. Without both of you, I would not have had the perspective to take on such an important topic. Thank you for giving me the platform to truly make a difference each day.

Finally, I thank my family and husband. I rely on their honest feedback to make sure I stay grounded and sane.

Over the years, I have had countless interactions with outstanding educators. Let's use the principles in this book to keep learning together for years to come.

About the Author

Kristen Swanson helps teachers design meaningful, interactive curricula at the local and national level. In the past she has taught at the elementary level, served as a regional consultant for Response to Intervention, and worked as an educational technology director for a public school district in Pennsylvania. She holds a B.A. degree from DeSales University, two M.A. degrees from Wilkes University, and an Ed.D. degree from Widener University. Kristen is currently an adjunct in the DeSales University instructional technology M.Ed program.

In addition to her experience as an educator, Kristen is also passionate about meaningful professional learning. She serves on the board of the Edcamp Foundation, a nonprofit organization designed to facilitate local, grassroots professional development. She has shared her ideas and expertise at an ASCD conference, TEDxPhiladelphiaEd, and Educon. She has also been published in academic journals, including *Literacy Learning: The Middle Years* and the *Journal of Reading, Writing, and Literacy*.

Kristen is active in the educational technology sphere. She is a Google Certified Teacher, Twitter Teacher, Edublog Award Nominee, and avid blogger. She strongly believes that strong curriculum fosters meaningful technology integration, and she is also interested in the learning opportunities provided by asynchronous learning.

Contents

Introduction

Ownership doesn't have to be equity or even control. Ownership comes from understanding and from having the power to make things happen.
—Seth Godin

At the beginning of my career, there was a lovely teacher across the hall from me. She was perfect. She always managed to arrive early, she completed her lesson plans with ease each day after school in a matter of minutes, and she NEVER jammed the copier. Her students loved her, and her teaching seemed effortless. To top it all off, she was calm in all situations and parents respected her. Of course, by October of my first year, *I secretly hated her.* In my classroom, things were not going nearly as smoothly. Kids acted out, I accidentally copied the wrong graphic organizers, and my lesson plans took me until 6 p.m.! What was I doing wrong? (Or perhaps, conversely, was I doing anything right?)

As time went on, I began to wonder how she had reached a state of such perfection. First, I considered her lineage. Maybe she was a relation of Mother Teresa or Jaime Escalante. After learning that she was simply the granddaughter of a fine Pennsylvania Dutch woman, I jumped to the next obvious conclusion: she was just a "born teacher"—one of those little girls who "played school" for her entire childhood followed by countless summer camp counselor jobs and hospital volunteer work.

Well, it turns out that I'm not alone in my conjectures about superior teachers. Most researchers, teachers, parents, and community members assume that gifted teachers were fashioned innately in the womb. However, research from the 21st Century Teaching Project reveals that none of the award-winning teachers selected for the study described themselves as having a clear understanding of best practices at the beginnings of their careers (Dikkers, 2012). Instead, award-winning teachers described themselves as starting with "faulty beliefs" about teaching and learning that they corrected through observing exemplars and interacting in a professional community. In fact, 33 percent of award-winning teachers in the study cited a specific moment when they realized that they were "doing it all wrong," and this served as their impetus for improvement and professional development (Dikkers, 2012).

It is a widely held belief that the professional learning cycle looks something like this:

professional development session

⊍

teacher learning

⊍

increased student achievement

Instead, it appears that the cycle looks like this:

frustration

⊍

teacher learning

⊍

increased student achievement

This is not to say that teachers don't benefit from professional development sessions offered by their schools. In many cases, they do. However, most teachers have to experience that "AHHHHHH moment" (much angrier than the traditional "aha moment") when they begin to repudiate faulty, comfortable practices *before* such sessions have much effect.

Further, most successful teachers learn from a combination of resources, including local communities, virtual communities, and research. The road to teacher proficiency is diverse and varied. Sadly, there's not a magic formula or prescriptive program that will raise the overall effectiveness of your practice. Instead, you need to become a curious learner who researches and collaborates with teachers at large.

Let's return to my amazing teaching neighbor for a second. One day I knew that the student groupings during math just weren't working in my classroom. (Read: My "AHHHHHH moment.") At the end of the day, I stormed across the hall and asked, "Okay, what's your secret?" Sensing my frustration, she told me to sit down and poured me a cup of tea. She explained that she had had a teaching mentor when she first started who shaped her beliefs about teaching. She also said that her first year of teaching had been incredibly difficult. (At this, I sighed with relief.) Then, suddenly, she pulled out her lesson plan book and asked, "Would you like to plan with me this week?" And with that, we became fast professional friends. We planned together and learned from each other. We brought in articles from professional journals, team-taught together, and even shared dessert recipes. As time passed, I began to realize that her classroom was filled with little experiments that informed her practice. While each activity was based on best practices, she carefully evaluated the results to consider if they were worth continuing. She was reflective, and she was never afraid to admit failure. Most importantly, she gave me a model and exemplar. In essence, working with her was my very first attempt at becoming an active, self-sufficient learner. Our students directly benefited from our work. As my teaching improved, so did my student outcomes. Remember, *teachers* are the number one factor affecting student achievement!

If you're reading this book, I'm hopeful that you're ready to make a change in your practice or your habits. Maybe you've even had your "AHHHHHH moment" recently. I'm also hopeful that you come in search of an outlet for your creativity, passion, and curiosity about teaching. The purpose of this book is to provide you with a series of tools and strategies (both virtual and in person) for meaningful professional development that can be shared throughout your school, your district, your local community, and the global online space. Consider the book to be an introduction to a community of learners much like yourself. None of the solutions provided in this book is a quick fix or simple tweak. Each requires a redirection of your current efforts and an application of your talents. However, the rewards will be bountiful. Once you take control of your own professional learning, you will be energized and amazed by the powerful, generous colleagues you have across this planet. Dig in. Power up. Connect!

How to Read This Book

I wrote this book to provide you, the learner, with an easy-to-follow resource guide to help you realize the power of both physical and virtual learning communities. Each chapter includes practical teacher cases, face-to-face protocols, tech tools, research snippets, and key ideas. Look for the icons below to help you navigate the text.

Educator Cases

This icon signals an educator's story or experience related to the topic or chapter at hand. It will describe, in detail, how an educator faced a problem, addressed it, and moved forward. These cases also serve as good discussion fodder at faculty meetings or department meetings.

Face-to-Face Protocols

While most learning opportunities in this book relate to learning in virtual or online spaces, there are also times when face-to-face interactions fit your needs as a learner. This icon will denote these protocols and suggestions.

Research Snippets

This book strives not only to give you practical tools and tips to accelerate your professional learning in both physical and online spaces, but also to share research that supports digitized learning. When you see this icon, you are hitting a "research section" in the book. If you're not interested in the research, feel free to skip over the section.

Key Ideas

This icon alerts you to a key idea in the text. It means that what's contained in the adjacent passage is critical to understanding social, digital learning.

To-Do Lists

This icon (at the end of each chapter) coincides with a to-do list. One of the most frustrating things about trying something new is figuring out where to start. Each list gives you three to five actionable steps to move you forward in your journey toward user-generated learning.

Defining User-Generated Learning

Professional development at my school is like pudding.
It can be sweet and delicious, or weird and bread.
—Anonymous

Meet Angelina

Angelina was a first-grade teacher in Los Angeles. Her class was a bustling melting pot: she taught students from seven different countries. A few of her students did not speak English, and several had individualized education plans. Each week, a consultant came to her school. During her prep period, the consultant helped Angelina revise and refine her lesson plans and units. While this type of support was helpful, it didn't meet all of Angelina's needs. Angelina was still struggling to differentiate her lessons to meet the needs of *all* her students. Angelina really needed to connect with other educators who were successfully reaching their English language learners and special education populations.

One day, while Angelina was surfing the web for examples of idioms to share with her students, she found a collaborative project called the Winter Wonderland Wiki. The wiki was looking for classrooms across the nation to work together on an interdisciplinary project. Students would post poems, drawings, and temperature measurements in their towns or cities, creating a global exchange about winter. As Angelina navigated the site, she realized that a teacher, just like her, was running the site. Feeling brave and a bit reckless, she fired off an e-mail to the organizer.

Within a few hours, she had a response from Mary, the organizer of the project. Mary taught second grade at an elementary school in New Jersey. Mary asked Angelina if she'd like to Skype to learn more about the project and how to set it up.

They set a time to Skype, and soon Mary's class was showing Angelina's class how to add to the project. Angelina's class was really excited to work with students across the country. One of Angelina's first graders "just couldn't believe" that it was *so* cold in New Jersey!

Before long, Mary and Angelina were exchanging e-mails regularly. Mary encouraged Angelina to join Twitter and follow other educators in the group. Although Twitter had always seemed silly to Angelina, she trusted Mary and signed up. Before long, Angelina was checking out a daily stream of lesson ideas and tools to use with her students.

To organize all the sites and resources that she found on Twitter, she started using Pearltrees. She would see a cool resource on Twitter, click on it, and then use the Pearltree button on her browser to save it. Pearltrees helped Angelina make collections of websites so that she and her students could easily find the games, animal information sites, and kid-friendly news sources during guided reading or math practice time. All the sites were saved online, so she could get to her resources from anywhere. Angelina's students were really excited each time she unveiled a new Pearltree in class, and many of the students' parents started using the resources at home as well.

After about six months, Angelina was feeling very comfortable curating digital resources and sharing them with other people she followed on Twitter. Several colleagues started to notice that things were changing in Angelina's classroom, and they asked how they could get involved. Before long, Angelina was sharing her websites, tips, and tricks with almost every-one in her school.

Angelina chose to take a risk and reach out to another educator on the web. The new connection not only made her a better teacher but also made her a better learner. Angelina is one of the many teachers who have turned to user-generated learning to improve their practice.

What Is User-Generated Learning?

User-generated learning is learning acquired through active curation, reflection, and contribution to a self-selected collaborative space. This basically means that user-generated learning is something you *do*, not something you get. You have to actively participate in the process through searching, evaluating, and sharing. In user-generated learning, everyone has something to contribute. We are all experts in our own ways. This doesn't negate the importance of educational research or vetted practices. Instead, user-generated learning reflects that all adults recognize their personal applications of ideas and strategies, and this synthesis and community are a valuable part of the learning process.

Let's break down each part of the definition provided above. First, user-generated learning requires curation. Curation is defined as the careful collection of relevant resources. Just like a museum employee, teachers must find and aggregate content that is relevant to the problems they are facing in their profession. Need resources for a new unit you are teaching? Interested in trying guided reading during your reading block? Need fun sites for students to use to practice mitosis and meiosis? Curation can help! Instead of relying on a content area expert or textbook, you are responsible for

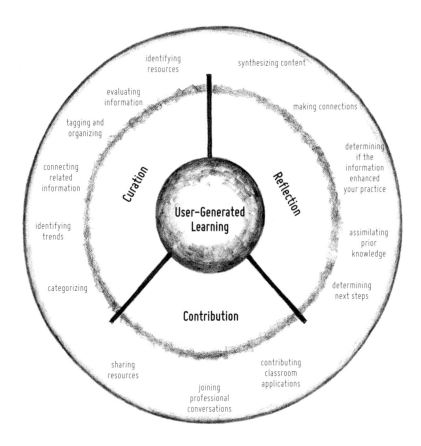

finding meaningful information. Curation can occur in many forms, such as using file folders, saving pages from professional journals, or copying article excerpts to share with colleagues. However, the Internet provides fantastic new tools that allow you to find, organize, and share content in ways that were previously not possible. Further, using online tools such as Twitter, Google Reader, Pearltrees, iTunes U, and Paper. li fosters sharing. You benefit greatly from what the community selects and shares. The community essentially serves as a functional filter to help you find the best content. By using the Internet to learn from lots of teachers, not just the teachers where you work, you will find better solutions that meet your students' needs. For example, maybe you are having difficulty engaging your students with a very traditional poetry unit that you have always taught. Curation can help you skim and search lots of different educational blogs each day for ideas. Perhaps your curation leads you to the FlickrPoet site (www .storiesinflight.com/flickrpoet/), where students can write poems and aggregate images for each word. Before long, you have students writing haiku poetry, creating really powerful visuals, and sharing their work with the school community. The right resource at the right time can really help you make a positive change for the students in your classroom.

Many of the chapters of this book were researched using my own personal system of content curation that includes Twitter, Paper.Li, and Google Reader. Later chapters of this book will focus on all these tools, and I will share some of the tips and tricks I've learned, aiding your pursuit of user-generated learning.

Reflection is the second component of user-generated learning. As you curate and consume information from a variety of sources, you must take the time to assimilate the new information with your existing background knowledge. Sometimes the information you've curated will match what you already know. Other times, it will challenge previously held beliefs. (A good curator always includes a variety of viewpoints when aggregating content.) As you wrestle with the information relative to your beliefs, your reflection will be critical. Just as there are many ways to curate, there are also many ways to reflect. You could simply write your thoughts in a small journal or word-processing document. However, you could also start your own online blog, allowing others in your learning community to comment on your reflections. Blogs are dynamic spaces for transactional, or interactive, reflection. Personally, the feedback, questions, and comments I've received on my blog (www.kristenswanson.org) have both affirmed my beliefs and challenged me as a learner. Reflection tools will be discussed in more detail in Chapter 3.

Third, user-generated learning requires a contribution to the learning community that you serve. You can select a community from physical or virtual places. At the local level, you could connect with your grade-level team, department, school, or district. At the virtual level, you could join an online forum, create a list of followers on Twitter, or identify and follow your favorite blog writers. Some people contribute to both physical and virtual communities. I contribute to both the schools where I work as well as the Twitter hashtag #edcamp. (Don't worry . . . there is more information on hashtags and Twitter coming up!) Both communities are important to me as a learner, and I try to share resources with both groups at least twice a week. That's a frequency that is manageable for me, but other people contribute on completely different schedules. As this is an individualized system, that is perfectly A-Okay!

User-generated learning is thus a three-part process: curation, reflection, and contribution. Each phase can be distinct or they can overlap. Certainly, user-generated learning is not linear or clean. It's messy. The more you become engaged with it, the harder it is to see clear distinctions between the phases. This book will explore each part of the process, providing you with tools and strategies to match your learning needs. Many times, the needs of your students or your role also drive the process. Do you teach middle schoolers? Then your Twitter list or Google Reader might include lots of middle school teachers and blogs to help you find engaging nonfiction texts geared to middle school students. (Middle school teachers typically know that anything gross, weird, or scary will get their kids' attention right away!) Are you a school principal? Then perhaps you follow thought leaders in both business and education to help you implement your vision. You could borrow inspirational quotes from your Twitter stream for your weekly school newsletter and post pictures from school events online. Maybe you're a preservice teacher? If so, then follow *everyone* in education and ask lots of questions to help you find your niche!

Consider the profile of "a day in the life" of an educator who practices user-generated learning (page 10). You can see that both online tools and face-to-face connections shape this teacher's classroom and teaching.

View the suggestions about this process as a buffet. Some things will fit your personality and work habits better than others. Also, some strategies are particularly suited to certain topics or subjects. Again, you are in control. You are the professional. If a strategy is not meeting your needs, change it!

It should be noted that the idea of user-generated learning provided in this book is heavily supported by the leading research on adult learning. That is why the strategies in this book are so successful for so many people. User-generated learning simply matches what we already know about adults and professional learning.

A Quick Recap of Adult Learning Theory

Research on adult learning shows that purpose, relevance, and immediacy are important to adult learners. For adult learning experiences to be successful, learners should be aware of the intention of the activity. Instruction should be problem-based instead of content-based, and planning should be collaborative. Succinctly, adults must be engaged with the content and one another to accomplish vital tasks.

Malcolm Knowles's theory of andragogy emphasizes that adult learners are self-directed (Knowles, Holton, & Swanson, 1998). They must be recognized and respected for their life experiences; positive relationships can augment the learning process. Moore and Kearsley (2004) echo this need for "closeness," especially in virtual or online environments. Termed transactional distance, the concept describes the distance between individuals in online environments. The primary

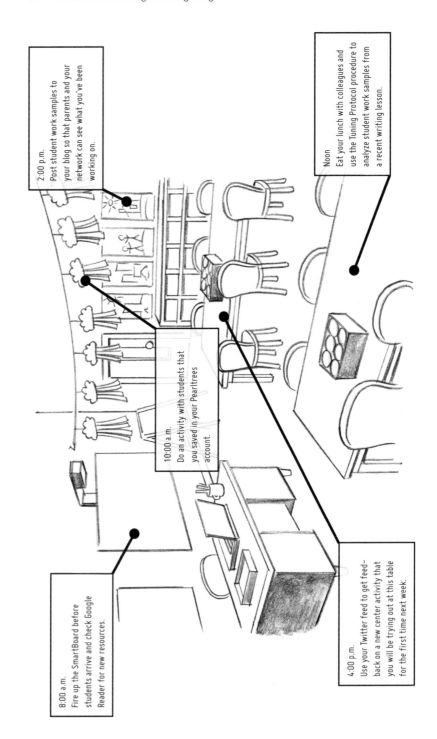

2:00 p.m.
Post student work samples to your blog so that parents and your network can see what you've been working on.

Noon
Eat your lunch with colleagues and use the Tuning Protocol procedure to analyze student work samples from a recent writing lesson.

10:00 a.m.
Do an activity with students that you saved in your Pearltrees account.

8:00 a.m.
Fire up the SmartBoard before students arrive and check Google Reader for new resources.

4:00 p.m.
Use your Twitter feed to get feedback on a new center activity that you will be trying out at this table for the first time next week.

method for lessening distance is dialogue. The more people interact via discussion boards, e-mail, and video chat, the less distance they perceive. Adults thrive in learning environments where they feel connected to both the task and the related individuals.

In his book *Drive*, Daniel Pink (2011) cites autonomy, mastery, and purpose as the three components of establishing motivation. The typical rewards, such as money, do not motivate adults to perform at their best. Instead, giving adults the freedom to choose, problem-solve, and have control seems to produce much greater results. In his book, Pink cites research that clearly indicates that higher levels of cognition are not motivated by external rewards. Instead, people who were not offered rewards for tasks that involved more than rote, mechanical skill performed better, persevered longer, and generally experienced higher levels of success. User-generated learning is a personal process driven by you, the teacher. As I write this book, there are currently no formal structures in place to reward or sanction this type of learning. However, that probably works in our favor to motivate lasting, meaningful cognition. Remember the roaring lion at the end of MGM movies? Right below the lion it said, "Ars Gratia Artis." This means "Art for Its Own Sake." Equally so, it is knowledge for its own sake (and the sake of our learners!) that drives user-generated learning.

User-generated learning is a three-phase process that honors the tenets of the research on adult learning. You can participate in user-generated learning anytime, anywhere. It is "on demand" and topics are self-selected. Further, user-generated learning is most successful when it is experienced in the context of a community, whether physical or virtual, with strong connections between the members. User-generated learning is also highly personalized. People may engage in this activity differently based on their preferences or learning styles. This variety is not merely expected; it is encouraged.

Where Does User-Generated Learning Take Place?

User-generated learning is space agnostic. That is a fancy way of saying that you can engage in this type of learning anytime, anywhere. More practically, you can engage in user-generated learning at your school during a grade-level meeting, faculty meeting, or professional development day. You can also engage in user-generated learning on a Saturday morning in your pajamas while checking sites from which you curate or while composing a blog post. The space, time, and format are up to you. If the culture of the institution where you work or study is not yet prepared to engage in user-generated learning (that is, it still requires you to participate in whole-group mandated trainings that are wholly unlinked to your practice for three in-service days a year), then I strongly encourage you to test out the online space as a vehicle for your user-generated learning.

Personally, I am a strong advocate for user-generated learning in the online space. The online space offers you the unique opportunity to collect information from educators across the nation and the globe. Also, it provides you with greater access to colleagues and experts who can craft and shape your thinking. Students benefit when the learning events you select have been tried by thousands of educators across the globe. Notably, there are many free tools that can assist your professional learning.

The Growth of Online Learning

More and more learning is moving online. In a report called *Learning on Demand*, Allen and Seaman (2009) report that online learning environments are quickly outpacing traditional learning environments: "Online enrollments have continued to grow at rates far in excess of the total higher education student population, with the most recent data showing no signs of slowing." There are varied reasons for this growth, including convenience, increased access to high-speed networks, and the growing demands in the workplace for lifelong learning. As a teacher, you should recognize that you probably will be expected to participate, either formally or informally, in these learning spaces at some point in the future. Further, your students will also be expected to utilize these spaces after they leave school. Your familiarity and comfort with the online space as a learning environment is critical to your ability to adequately prepare students for the future.

In 2011 the International Society of Technology in Education (ISTE) released a white paper called *Technology, Coaching, and Community*. The summation of the paper includes ten items for leveraging technology, coaching, and community. The first item on the list is: "Learning with technology is more important than learning about technology" (Beglau et al., 2011, p. 16). If you are going to adequately prepare students for modern, technology-rich workplaces, you must be comfortable learning in online spaces yourself. Learning, making mistakes, and experimenting in the online space not only provides meaningful professional content but also gives you the opportunity to experience successful, technology-rich educational environments.

In his book *Cognitive Surplus*, Clay Shirky reminds us that we all have the time and expertise to contribute to learning communities. Contributions are growing all the time. Humans prefer to be actively engaged during their free time, not passively entertained. However, many Americans are not engaged yet. Shirky notes that "Americans watch roughly two hundred billion hours of TV every year. That represents about two thousand Wikipedias' projects' worth of free time annually" (2010, p. 157). So perhaps we do have the time. Garrison Keillor is fond of saying, "We have all the time there is." Perhaps we do have the autonomy and competence to use user-generated learning to enhance our professional learning and development.

Remember Angelina?

Individuals who are currently practicing user-generated learning strategies report that they are looking for information and development beyond what is available immediately in their schools. Essentially, they are finding what's outside their classroom "box." Remember Angelina from the beginning of this chapter? She was looking for something beyond what her school was able to provide. She was looking for connections with educators like herself as well as organizational structures that could help her use resources more effectively. Through her connection with Mary and the Winter Wonderland Wiki, Angelina was able to create a system that provided her students with rich resources. She also made professional friends with many people, both in real life and virtually, during the process. User-generated learning helped Angelina be more successful in her classroom.

The following chapters in this book will explore each phase of user-generated learning: curation, reflection, and contribution. Just as each phase of user-generated learning is not clearly distinct, these chapters do not need to be read in order. You are encouraged to skip to topics that suit your immediate needs or interests. As you read each chapter, try out some of the strategies or ideas that appeal to you. Using this text as a reference and resource will prove more valuable than simply reading the entire body of work straight through.

Your To-Do List

1. **Make sure you have a computer with an Internet connection.** (No computer? No problem! Try your local library or your school computer lab.)
2. **Identify the types of benefits you want to gain from user-generated learning.** Do you want to talk with other educators who teach the same grade or subject you do? Or perhaps you'd like to find relevant websites to include in your instruction? Moving forward with a specific goal can make the process seem more manageable.
3. **Find a friend.** User-generated learning is so much easier with a buddy! Consider approaching a colleague to join you on this journey.

Curation

Empowerment means establishing a culture in which people are hungry for evidence and are willing to face the brutal facts when things don't work out as hoped.
—DuFour and Marzano

Meet Mathieu Plourde

Mathieu Plourde was an educational technologist working for the University of Delaware. Although incredibly smart colleagues surrounded him on campus, he felt that he needed to regularly talk with people who were exploring the same technologies and techniques to improve teaching and learning as he was, specifically helping faculty members adapt skills to their own contexts. He needed to find resources that other people in his field were using. In short, how could he find the best tools, especially if they didn't show up in a simple Google search?

In 2008, Mathieu attended the EDUCAUSE Learning Initiative educational conference in San Antonio, Texas. He met many people who were investigating and exploring many of the problems and issues he faced in his work. Many of the conference-goers were using Twitter as a back channel at the conference. Mathieu signed up, started following all the people he had met at the conference, and watched the information start rolling in. When asked about this experience, he said, "It was the first time I'd used any social media service like that. The people I connected with when I created my account were all in the same field as me."

Over time, Mathieu started using Twitter more and more. Soon he needed a way to save and organize all the links, conversations, and posts that Twitter was delivering. He tried several different tools before settling on Diigo. Diigo allowed him to organize and save all the links that he was finding and sharing. Whenever Mathieu saw something in his Twitter stream that seemed interesting, he opened the link and clicked his Diigo bookmark tool. Using this simple process, he could save this link in different categories, or tags. Mathieu was able to easily retrieve these resources, shared by people "in his shoes," to enhance his work with colleagues and faculty members. The professors with whom he worked were amazed by his seemingly endless supply of tools and resources. Before long, Mathieu couldn't remember his professional life before user-generated learning.

Curation Is Not a New Idea

In the past, curating was relatively easy. Teachers, known fondly to their families and friends as pack rats, filed and saved just about every piece of paper they could find. Worksheets, memos, and articles were crammed into color-coded files near the back of the classroom.

During my student teaching, I knew a teacher who planned to retire in June. I distinctly remember the day she "gave me her files." This seemed like such a boon! I greedily carried boxes and boxes of endless science articles, *Time* magazines, and Edhelper worksheets to my car. At the time I thought there was nothing more valuable in the world.

Such collections of valuable resources were not readily available at that time. Teachers were zealous about protecting their materials. Therefore, the act of curation in the past was largely individual (as was the act of teaching itself). Teachers were left to their own devices to find, aggregate, and retain meaningful resources about their practice. This led to over-stuffed classrooms with teachers who were constantly wondering, "Where did I put THAT?"

While the old ways of curation still hold their value, they are far less likely to provide you with a thorough, interactive system for personalized learning. Opening your eyes to the new ways of curation can greatly enhance the tools, tips, and strategies at your fingertips.

New Ways of Curation

Today's curation is completely different. Most importantly, it is highly social. Teachers can share their collections with each other effortlessly, making the quality and quantity of resources available to new teachers and new curators much more robust than in the past.

In the modern model of curation, teachers can provide feedback to each other as they curate their resources. It is easy to organize resources and links and sites. You don't need to be a web designer or techno-geek to take advantage of modern tech tools. They are often free, easy to use, and constantly improving.

The other game changer in modern curation is the fact that services exist to deliver relevant content *to you*. No longer are you required to actively find relevant content or information. You simply wait for it to show up. With the right searches, feeds, and tweets, you can amass an amazing amount of relevant content in a short period of time. To give you an idea of the potential that exists, my Google Reader page typically has about 200 new items each day!

In fact, it is quite common for new curators to be over-whelmed by the number of tools and tips they receive each day. Often the amount of information is discouraging. Don't be discouraged. You don't have to read everything. Just make sure that everything you value is tagged and organized appro-priately. If you can't get back to the information, then it doesn't matter that you found it in the first place.

When entering the new world of curation, there are three typical steps that you must follow: aggregate, evaluate, and organize.

Aggregation

Aggregation is defined by the Merriam-Webster dictionary as "the collecting of units or parts into a mass or whole." For teachers who are seeking to engage in user-generated learn-ing, aggregation helps them amass content that is useful to their students and their classrooms. Instead of reactively searching Google every time they need a resource, they have content delivered to them daily. When a need arises, they look in their archives of filtered content and select what they need. This is the easiest part of the curation process because today's networked culture has produced very large quantities of rel-evant information. (There are also mountains of irrelevant information—avoiding them can be a challenge!)

Your first step is to identify a content aggregator that works for you. My favorites are Twitter, Paper.li, Google Reader, Flip-board, Zite, and iTunes U. They are all free, and they all have the ability to deliver customized content based on your prefer-ences. Please see Tool Repository A at the end of this book for a full review of each tool with step-by-step instructions.

Here are a few very specific examples of how aggregation works:

Problem: Denise is teaching a new unit on space exploration and needs to find resources.

Solution: At the recommendation of her colleague, Denise goes to http://reader.google.com and signs up for a free account. Next, she clicks on the "subscribe" button and enters in the web addresses of a few of her favorite NASA and space sites. Denise also checks Tool Repository C in this book and finds a few educational tools and video blogs to add as well. Each morning, she checks her account and tags resources that look useful. Denise is able to share these resources with her students very easily using the "share" function inside Google Reader. Before long, Denise's students are walking into the classroom asking her, "What cool stuff did you find today?"

Problem: Mark needs to find an engaging activity for his students to work on over the holiday break.

Solution: Mark posts his question to Twitter, and within minutes several teachers respond with activities and ideas. He clicks on the links they shared. (He knows the links are for him because they are in his "mentions" column.) He chooses his favorite, downloads it, prints it for his students, and goes to class. His students really like the challenging problems he has provided for them, and over 80 percent of the class (a much higher percentage than usual!) completes the holiday work.

Evaluation

Evaluation is the second step of curation. Once all the content is delivered to you, you have to determine what you are going to do with it. Remember, you don't have to keep everything you find! (NOTE: The entire section that follows will not only help *you* evaluate but also help your *students* evaluate information they find online. Feel free to try these suggestions and tools with your students as they perform Internet research.)

The power of aggregation and the World Wide Web will deliver a large repository of information to you. However, users just like you create most of that information. So how do you know what's worth hanging onto? Well, you need to hone your crap detection skills. This term originates from an Ernest Hemingway quote in 1965: "Every man should have a built-in automatic crap-detector operating inside him." This phrase has been made popular again by several leading minds in online learning, especially Howard Rheingold (2009). Evaluating aggregated content is not only a vital skill for your professional learning but also a fundamental skill to teach to your students.

Howard Rheingold offers several methods to evaluate sources and "detect crap." Most importantly, he urges learners and searchers to identify the author or source of the information. Although the author's identity is not always obvious, it can usually be determined by checking the footer of the webpage or post. In addition to seeking credible sources, Rheingold offers a variety of sites and services that can assist the evaluation process for learners:

+ http://easywhois.com finds the author of a particular site.
+ http://factcheck.org identifies myths and hoaxes.

Don't be fooled by the appearance of a site. It is possible to make an extremely professional-looking site with a limited amount of knowledge. It is best to triangulate your information. Look for various sources that say the same thing. Check the author, see if others are bookmarking the site, and double-check the information at http://factcheck.org. Acting like a detective is an essential strategy and life skill when you are generating your own learning.

The University of Maryland also offers a fantastic web-based website credibility checklist. Check it out here: www.lib .umd.edu/guides/webcheck.html. My "quick five question" credibility quiz for websites also guides my browsing and evaluation. Every time I visit a site, I ask myself the following five questions:

1. **Who created or wrote the content on the site?** Is the author a person, a company, a nonprofit, a university? Do I consider the source credible? An easy way (which is *not*, however, 100 percent foolproof) to check the source is to notice the last three letters of the web address: for example, .com = company, .org = organization/nonprofit, .edu = university, .gov = government.
2. **What is the purpose of the website?** Is the author trying to inform me, persuade me, sell something to me? Does the intention represent a bias of some sort?
3. **How up-to-date is the website?** When was the last time the site was updated? Is content added regularly? Are revisions time-stamped? A "fresh site" with active streams of content is often more reliable than a "dead site" that is never updated.
4. **Does the site have links or citations to other credible sources?** Is the site transparent about where its information comes from? Do the site's creators triangulate their sources using either websites or books?
5. **Can I contact the webmaster or author?** Can I access the person who created this content and get a response?

People who are willing to engage in dialogue about their work often make large efforts to ensure their work is credible.

It's also important to note that relationships and trust in online spaces assist the evaluation process. Those of you who are new to the online world may be shaking your heads. Trust in the online space?? No way! However, the world of educational bloggers is very personal and interconnected. I have met many of the writers that I aggregate in my Google Reader in person.

For example, I met Richard Byrne, the amazing author of *Free Tech for Teachers*, at a Google Certified Teacher Academy. He was very humble and gracious, and we managed to connect on Twitter following the event. I've written guest blog posts for him, asked him questions, and replied to his tweets. I know that he is an educator engaged in the same learning process that I am, and that lends a lot of credibility to his work. These types of relationships form more easily than you may currently realize.

And while I recognize that it's not practical to assume that you can meet every educational blogger you follow, it *is* practical to assume that you can engage them through their work. When I leave blog comments and receive insightful responses from the author, the exchange lends credibility to the content on the page. Building relationships in online spaces can certainly help you to identify which tweets, posts, and articles are most accurate and most relevant.

I must admit that this advice is counterintuitive to most practicing teachers. We've been taught for generations that meaningful content is corralled in academic journals and libraries. I do still believe this is true to an extent. However, there is rich learning that extends beyond those boundaries. I want to learn and interact with interesting ideas and interesting people every day of my life. Online spaces certainly make that more possible than ever before.

Evaluation is something that will continue to grow and evolve as the content on the web changes. New strategies will rise and fall just as content aggregators will wax and wane.

Organization (Tagging)

So you've aggregated content, you've reviewed and evaluated it, and you like it. Now what? Well, you have to put it away, of course! The organization of digital resources can be extremely fluid and flexible. Teachers can quickly assign tags or folders to the content they find. Tags are like labels that you can assign to different pieces of content. In some ways, tags are like the folders on your traditional desktop computer. However, tags are more flexible and more efficient than traditional folders for one very important reason. Unlike the organization of documents or files on a traditional computer, multiple tags can be assigned to the same piece of content, allowing users to make a variety of neural connections, which enhances recall.

Let's consider a closet analogy. Just imagine if you could organize your closet by clothing type (skirt, shirt, sweater, etc.) and your favorite outfit combinations (best suit set, favorite race day gear, etc.) *at the same time*. Amazing. You could change the way you search based on the problem you're trying to solve. Effective tagging makes it a reality for your online resources.

For example, if I decide to put www.starfall.com in my "literacy resources" tag, that's certainly a step in the right direction. However, if I tag www.starfall.com in the "literacy resources," "phonics," and "smartboard" tags, I'm much more likely to retrieve it in a variety of applied situations. As a teacher, I look for resources at different times for different reasons. By applying multiple tags to my best content, I can easily find it again at the appropriate times.

Tags look different based on the aggregation service that you use, but they all function the same way. They serve as a map of your meaning-making process.

One thing that's important to note is that tags can be highly personal. My list of tags may look completely different from my colleagues' tags. That's okay. Remember, user-generated learning is a highly individualized process. There is, however, one situation in which you may want to consider sticking to a list of tags. If you are working on a research project or unit collaboratively with a group of teachers, you may want to determine your tags *before* you start aggregating and evaluating content. If you all use the same tags, it will be much easier to pull information together in a streamlined, coherent way. I often use this strategy when working with students in a class. But when it comes to my personal learning and my personal projects, my tags follow a highly individualized pattern.

For a step-by-step review of different ways to tag inside aggregation services, see Tool Repository D.

Curation Gives Us a Voice

Consider this. Fred McClimans wrote a blog post detailing the 12 most disruptive business issues for 2012. One of the issues was "The Consumer as Boss." In the past, the consumer was required to accept what was available with little voice in the process. Unless consumers were included in a focus group or special feedback committee, their voices were largely unheard by those who create, produce, and write. Today the advent of both social media and blogging has allowed everyday consumers to have a voice. You, as a curator, have the right not only to evaluate but also to publicly share your thoughts, tips, and strategies. So put yourself in control. You have a say in what you consume, what is delivered to you, and what you choose to assimilate into your practice. You are living in an incredibly interactive time, and information is a tradable currency.

It's important to remember that our students have grown up in a fully participatory world. Although the idea of "Consumer as Boss" might be new to us, it is all that our students know. If we accept that premise, it leads us to understand why learning activities we select must be active, participatory, and democratic. Using tools found via curation can help us honor this notion held by our students.

One danger with curation is that you place yourself in an echo chamber of what you already believe. It is important to curate from a balanced selection of sources. A few things you read each day should contradict your existing beliefs. A clear understanding of multiple methods, pedagogies, and beliefs will only serve to strengthen your learning, understanding, and opinions.

Unlearning is hard. Breaking strongly held beliefs is very difficult due to the myriad cognitive connections that hold the information in place (i.e., the hangers in your closet). However, keeping an open mind and exposing yourself to lots of different ideas can make unlearning just a little bit easier.

Remember Mathieu?

Remember Mathieu? He's been curating his learning and connecting with colleagues online for years now. Mathieu cites the relevant conversations and the ability to connect to others with his specialties and interests as the motivation that keeps him "on that track." He says, "Everyone has a primary interest, and you never find people in your physical environment who have exactly the same interests as you. They are all

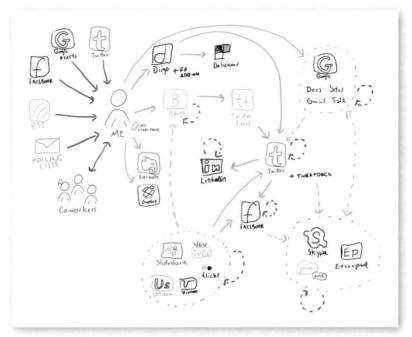

looking at something that's a little different. Adding access to that stream of consciousness online is valuable. The whole idea of curating is give and take."

Above is Mathieu's graphic depiction of his curation and sharing process. Note how diverse it is and how it relies on both physical and virtual networks.

Interested in meeting Mathieu and learning with him? Visit him on his blog, *Open Reflections* (http://mathplourde .wordpress.com).

The act of curation is highly engaging and highly active. As you engage in this process, remember to view the process as a buffet. You do not have to use every service, read every article, or tag every item. In fact, I don't recommend that at all! You'll never have enough time to sustain such an effort, and you'll get frustrated. You'll quit! Instead, choose just one or two ideas from this chapter at a time. Then revisit the chapter in a few months. It may spark an idea or two that you wish to implement. Remember, the path is not straight, and it is not clear. But it is wholly up to you.

Your To-Do List

1. **Sign up for Google Reader.** To begin curating, sign up for a free Google Reader account at http://reader .google.com. For screenshots and more information about Google Reader, check out Tool Repository A at the end of this book.
2. **Subscribe to ten blogs in Google Reader.** Using the "subscribe" button inside Google Reader, subscribe to ten websites or blogs relevant to your teaching. If you need suggestions on which blogs to follow, check out Tool Repository C at the end of this book.
3. **Click through the blog posts that appear inside Google Reader, evaluate them, and tag them.** When the posts load, review each one and tag it if you'd like to save it. Don't forget to use multiple tags on each item. For example, you might tag a math game with the following tags: "math," "games," and "smartboard."

Healthy Digital Footprints

A Vehicle for Curation

The secret to creativity is knowing how to hide your sources.
—Albert Einstein

Meet Patrick Larkin

Patrick Larkin was a high school administrator in Massachusetts. Each day, he was faced with challenging situations involving student technology and social media. Students were often punished for using cell phones during class, posting inappropriate pictures to Facebook, or cyberbullying one another at night through chats and websites. Patrick knew that many other administrators chose to ignore the issue or, even worse, required students to power down when they entered the school building. After lots of reading (via the curation tools in Chapter 3!), Patrick decided to take a different approach.

Instead of fearing social media and technology in school, he *embraced* it. Patrick signed up for Twitter and started a blog for his school. He asked students to help him throughout

NEXT YEAR's Musical

This entry was posted on April 13, 2012. Bookmark the permalink. 8 Comments

What Musical Should we do next year?

Many factors go into choosing the musical every year.

- As always, we try to select shows that will highlight the talent we have. (Some shows require a trained male dancer. I don't know any trained male dancers in the school).
- What shows will people want to come see? (this year's show was the lowest selling show in 5 years.)
- What shows will the students get excited about? (*Beauty & The Beast* had over 100 kids in the cast).
- What shows will the staff enjoy working on? (Someone on the staff should be passionate about the material we will have to spend months of time and energy on).
- What shows can feature a very large ensemble? (We have traditionally accepted everyone who auditions).
- What shows are appropriate for this age? (*RENT* would be very popular, but contains adult themes of drug use and sexual behavior which make many people very uncomfortable).
- What shows are available? (we must obtain the rights and pay royalties, many shows that are on Broadway such as *Wicked* are not available. *Chicago* is restricted, *Grease* is limited due to high demand).

If you have suggestions that you feel fit all of these categories, please feel free to send in your suggestions.

the project, and many of the students added content to the school blog each day. Content ranged from advertisements for upcoming social events to requests for suggestions about next year's musical. See the students' lively responses to Patrick's blog post on page 37.

In addition, Patrick engaged with his students on Twitter. Students tweeted him about their concerns, issues, and ideas. In most high schools, students don't have the opportunity to share ideas with the principal. Thanks to user-generated learning, Patrick's students can do this regularly. Now, students at Patrick's school have a strong digital role model: their principal.

Stephanie says:

April 16, 2012 at 7:39 pm

We should do high school musical

Reply

Marilyn says:

April 19, 2012 at 10:32 am

Bye Bye Birdie! Funny charachters, silly plot, lots of dancing, plenty of teenage extras! I think the kids will love the telephone scene! It will be fun for them to see how we communicated as teens!

Reply

David says:

April 19, 2012 at 10:35 am

Cats? (qualification: I've never seen it)

Reply

April says:

April 19, 2012 at 1:24 pm

Would love to see West Side Story! I don't think BHS has ever done it.

Reply

Stephanie says:

April 19, 2012 at 2:28 pm

West Side Story is a great idea. It does have a dance hall scene that can accomodate (probably) any number of actors.

Reply

Cathy says:

April 24, 2012 at 4:11 pm

Cats and West Side Story are both awesome choices.

Reply

B. says:

April 29, 2012 at 7:10 pm

Jesus Christ Superstar or Guys and Dolls?

Being Thoughtful About Digital Tools

Many of the curation methods recommended in this book rely on the use of digital tools. However, I caution you to tread carefully and thoughtfully when using new digital tools. To cite Bill Ferriter and Adam Garry, authors of *Teaching the iGeneration* (2010),

> To put it simply, human patterns for interacting with ideas are changing dramatically. Making sure that your students end up on the right side of this new digital divide starts with intentional efforts to introduce the kinds of tools, strategies, and behaviors that make information management, fluency, and evaluation easy. (p. 31)

However, the authors also state that using tools thoughtlessly will cause schools to miss the mark:

> Instead of recognizing that tomorrow's professions will require workers who are intellectually adept—able to identify bias, manage huge volumes of information, persuade, create, and adapt—teachers and district technology leaders wrongly believe that tomorrow's professions will require workers who know how to blog, use wikis, or create podcasts. As a result, schools sprint in new digital directions with little thought, spending thousands on technology before carefully defining the kinds of learning that they value most. The consequences are high-tech classrooms delivering meaningless, low-level instructional experiences. (p. 7)

It's clear that we must always frame the use of digital tools within the context of meaningful learning. When using the tools described in this chapter, always remember to ask yourself the following: *How* or *why* will this tool enhance my professional learning? If you can't answer that question for yourself, skip the tool.

Building Robust Professional Digital Footprints

Many teachers are afraid of their digital footprints, feeling that the only safe choice is to stay away from online portals. If you are using virtual spaces for professional learning, it only serves to enhance your digital footprint. Think about the modeling you could provide to your students, who often make poor, uninformed choices in digital spaces. We often chastise and reprimand students for making poor choices online. However, if there are no adults whom they know and respect in the online space, then the absence of viable models contributes to the problem. I once asked a preteen why she was publicly posting pictures from a recent slumber party. The response? "Well, everyone is doing it—who cares?" Although I was tempted to break out my grandmother's "jump off a bridge" taunt, I stopped and reflected upon the child's words. She was right. The only people in the online space were other naïve preteens. If adults were serving as models, their example would certainly assist children in making good decisions.

When I post online, I picture my grandmother and my boss reading the post *at the same time*. As long as I see a smile on both their faces, I press the post button. (NOTE: This strategy only works if your grandmother is *not* Betty White.)

Quantity Over Quality with Digital Footprints

We've been taught that quality, not quantity, is important. While I still agree that this is fundamentally true, it is not the way of the World Wide Web. Google searches, rankings, and other lists highly depend on the quantity of materials that users produce. While Google uses many different algorithms to produce what users are searching for, it was created based upon the number of sources linked to the page or site (Levy, 2011). This means that pages referenced frequently are more legitimate, more popular, and more likely to give you the answer you need. So what does this mean when you "Google yourself"? It means that the more legitimate content you've posted, the better. The more blog comments, webpages, and curation collections that are linked to your name, the more likely you are to achieve the goal of maintaining a positive digital footprint. If you've ever made a bad choice about posting something online, deleting it will not erase it from popular searches in Google or Bing. Your best defense is to post copious amounts of positive, intellectually stimulating material. Then your "mistake" will be buried by newer search results.

Joan was a first-year high school teacher in the Midwest. She was highly conservative, and she followed all the recommendations given to her by the university that she attended: stay off Facebook and don't post online. However, during her first few months on the job, Joan's students posted her picture on the infamous website *Hot or Not*, and soon students from the school were "rating" her. To add insult to injury, the posting was brought to Joan's attention by the parents of one of her students. Mortified, Joan told her principal about the situation. To Joan's horror, there was nothing the school could do about the incident because it had not happened during school time. Joan decided to talk to the school librarian, a huge fan of social media, to find out how to fix her situation. "Start a website, start a blog, and get on Twitter," recommended the librarian. That advice went against all of Joan's instincts. But since things couldn't get much worse, she decided to try it.

After a few months of positive posts about her teaching, the "Hot or Not" page was buried in search results for her name. It had almost (!) disappeared. Joan shared her experience with the staff at her school and teamed up with the school librarian to encourage all teachers to take control of the conversation about them online.

It's Okay to "Stalk"

It's likely that all this talk about posting appropriate things online is enough to make even the most dedicated teacher-learner a bit hesitant. It's okay to "stalk." This means that you take advantage of digital resources without actually posting anything. This is often a good method to use at first. Digital curation can be done relatively anonymously. Many teacher leaders are excited to share what they've learned with just about anyone. Most "stalkers" choose to jump into the fray after some time because they simply can't refrain from giving their input on a topic or blog post. And that's good!

Everything, Even Curation, Has a Season

Digital curation has become very popular in the last five years. One reason is that many teachers are embracing positive digital footprints and openly sharing their work. However, many other factors in digital and physical environments also contribute to the efficacy and desirability of aggregating, evaluating, and organizing content.

The Open Education Movement Supports Curation

Curation is reliant on the existence of freely available, high-quality content. In the past ten years, some of the most prestigious institutions and think tanks have started to publish their best material in free online spaces. Beginning in 2011, Stanford and Harvard offered several of their courses for free online (Colman, 2011). (Students don't receive credit, but they do have the opportunity to attend office hours with a professor.) Harvard even recently published video overviews of all its general education courses online (Harvard Program in General Education, 2012). (See them here: http://goo.gl/7FgcF).

Regarding open access in the scientific community, Michael Carroll (2011), a member of the Creative Commons board, wrote,

> Getting open access right matters because the new publishing model is designed to increase the pace and impact of scientific communication through the power of the Internet. Immediate, free publication increases the audience for scientific research and overcomes the increasingly high barrier to access imposed by the traditional, subscription based publishing model. (n.p.)

The open education movement is also growing beyond the walls of higher education. Sites such as P2PU (http://p2pu.org) give users access to free content, and they can run courses themselves. Sites like YouPD (http://youpd.org) use a "badge system" to help learners master complex instructional techniques and technology hacks.

It is clear that the open education movement strives to tear down the divides between the "information haves" and the "information have-nots." Because many people believe in unfettered access to knowledge, your curation will be deeper, richer, and more reliable. (The access to such high-quality content has deep ramifications for teaching—but that's another book!)

Curation Honors Brain Research

In the learning process, remembering, selecting, organizing, and categorizing are all essential parts. In her book *Design for How People Learn*, Julie Dirksen (2011) describes the brain as a closet. (I prefer to think of brains as really sophisticated walk-in closets bordered with fine oak . . .) Placing something on a shelf or hanger creates a pathway for you to recall the information in the future. Therefore, the act of curation forces your brain to create neural connections to specifically defined shelves in your brain. While this closet metaphor may be overly simplistic in many contexts, it certainly does explain why you remember exactly what you tagged or filed.

Think about it. How many times have you pictured exactly where the file folder was located in your cabinet even though you couldn't remember the contents of the file? Or perhaps you could visualize the page in the textbook that held the answer to the test question even though you could not remember the actual answer. These common experiences exhibit the power and strength of building cognitive schema while learning. Curating, tagging, and organizing provide your brain with multiple access points to the same content, allowing you to think flexibly and identify patterns.

The longer you curate, the more varied and complex your organization systems become. It's also not unusual for certain curation tools to wax and wane as you travel through your learning journey. As your interests change, so do your patterns of information management. Curation is the process by which you make meaning out of information in a brain-friendly way.

Remember Patrick?

Patrick is still using social media to help connect with his students in an appropriate way. Just recently, Patrick used Twitter with his students to celebrate "Poem in Your Pocket Day." Students shared their favorite poems via Twitter and built excitement for literacy within the learning community. See page 45 for a summary of his favorite submissions.

Think you can't get high school students engaged with poetry? Think again! Through the use of social media, Patrick has engaged his students and raised their opinion of the relevance of the art. His students see their school as a place that reflects the interactivity and connectivity that exists in their lives outside school. Meeting students where they are creates a healthy, productive educational climate.

Even better, Patrick has been able to create a seismic shift in the way that the media portray his school online. Instead of waiting to see what the local newspapers write about the school, Patrick has proactively partnered with local media outlets. The Burlington affiliate of the *Boston Globe* directly links to his Twitter feed and blog. Patrick has taken control of his school's digital footprint. Now he, not an uninformed reporter, is the author of the school's presence.

(9 Storify by **Patrick Larkin**   3 months ago

#PoemInPocket Recap

New Post: My #PocketPoem for Poem In Your Pocket Day bit.ly/Iq7lwU #bhschat

Patrick Larkin   3 months ago

The first poem I ever really got into was A Poison Tree by William Blake - a meditation on revenge online-literature.com/poe/622/ #pocketpoem #bhschat

Benjamin Lally   3 months ago

My favorite - "If called by a panther...don't anther."
Ogden Nash #bhschat #pocketpoem

Eric Conti   3 months ago

My fav poem: "Sick" by Shel Silverstein. Perfect for a day like today! #pocketpoem #bhschat
poets.org/viewmedia.php/prm...

Keith March Mistler   3 months ago

Happy Poem in Your Pocket Day! "Valentine for Ernest Mann" by Naomi Shihab Nye
uuwestport.org/Readings/val... #pocketpoem #bhschat

Stephanie Diozzi   3 months ago

Your To-Do List

1. **Google yourself.** Make sure you are logged out of all websites, and type your name into Google. See the results that pop up. Is there anything that makes you nervous? Any work you've done that you wish was more prominent? A simple Google search helps you see the most common information that others may find about you on the web.

2. **Learn how Google works.** Remember how quantity is more important than quality on the web? Learning how Google search works will explain this to you more clearly. Visit www.google.com/competition/howgooglesearchworks.html. Check out the videos and information. Understanding how Google search works should encourage you to post often to enhance your digital footprint.

3. **Check your privacy settings. On everything.** Are you a Facebook user? Perhaps you belong to another personal network. Log in to those services and check your privacy settings. Although privacy settings are never foolproof, checking them often can keep you in control of your digital footprint.

Reflection

*The self is not something ready-made, but something
in continuous formation through choice of action.*
—John Dewey

Meet Richard Byrne

Richard Byrne was a high school social studies teacher in Maine. Richard was an engaging teacher, and he honed his practice about sharing his classroom lessons, tips, and tools with others. After teaching for several years, he quickly realized that the best way to improve his lessons was to share his successes and shortcomings. One day, he decided to start a blog to share these musings with others.

He started by signing up for Blogger (www.blogger.com), a Google blog service. He then began to post about tools he was using in his classroom. At first, traffic to the site was slow, but it increased over time. Within a few months, people started leaving comments for Richard that pointed him to new tools and ideas. With that, he was off on a reflective learning journey!

Thinking About Reflection

Reflection is a natural part of teaching and learning. As we experience new things, we must make sense of them. After carefully curating information, we must take time to determine what the information means for our teaching practice.

Research has shown that educators who routinely reflect upon their practice produce better student outcomes. Teaching in isolation is one of the most persistent problems in improving schools today (Fulton, Yoon, & Lee, 2005). Reflection stems from a body of study about metacognition that dates back to the 1970s (Flavell, 1979). Metacognition, loosely termed "thinking about thinking," is a process in which people consider their own ideas, strategies, and strengths about both learning and teaching. Flavell says, "I am absolutely convinced that there is, overall, far too little rather than enough or too much cognitive monitoring in this world. This is true for adults as well as children" (p. 910).

Sometimes reflection can be difficult. Once configured correctly, curation becomes a type of automated task. It is also a rewarding task to check an inbox full of interesting content related to our professional interests. Further, our Pavlovian needs for feedback and fresh input condition us to respond to the beeps, buzzes, and chimes of our phones and computers without much difficulty. However, reflection is much different. It requires us to escape from the hectic pace of school and life. Given all the distractions that exist, finding time for reflection can be challenging. However, in spite of its difficulty, it is a task worth pursuing. Without reflection, we cannot make meaning or generate understandings from new information. Grant Wiggins and Jay McTighe (2005) champion this idea as part of their *Understanding by Design* framework. Essentially, as we manipulate new information in our minds, we can make connections and determine practical applications of the material. Patterns become apparent, allowing us to make generalizations that apply to our work. Just as this type of design benefits our students, it also benefits us as mature learners.

Although reflection has been traditionally described as a highly independent process, I believe that it is the precursor to productive sharing. Thoughtful reflection and articulation are the first step toward collaboration. Until we are comfortable with what happens inside our own classrooms and our own minds, we are not able to share with others. We must question what motivates our work and be able to describe it to others in a way that makes sense.

It's also important to remember that being transparent about our successes and struggles is an important behavior to model for our students. It's tempting to want students to see us, their teachers, as absolute experts or perfect persons. However, that's not reality. By blogging about the things that happen inside the classroom, we can create a culture of openness with our students. Katie Zorzi, a kindergarten teacher, wanted to share her classroom joy with her parents and community. She started a website (http://katiezorzi.posterous.com/) and students started taking pictures and writing brief content for the blog during their Kidwriting lessons. Before long, the site had hundreds of subscribers and thousands of views. What an easy way to share the learning journey with teachers, students, and parents!

The ability to share and transfer knowledge relies heavily on automaticity and facility with the information. Reflection provides this comfort, augmenting our ability to teach or share.

Ways to Reflect Upon Your Practice

As you begin user-generated learning, reflection may be a bit difficult to undertake. What, exactly, do you reflect upon? How do you know how much to write? Do you even have to write your reflections? These are all excellent questions. And, as I've stated before, user-generated learning is a highly personal process that differs from individual to individual. However, a few guidelines never hurt anyone. So I'm going to propose a number of strategies, topics, or tips that you could use to jump-start your professional reflection.

Try a strategy, tip, or tool that you found from your curated material and evaluate how it went. You will find a plethora of lesson ideas, tools, and tips as you curate content. Two places where I regularly find lesson ideas are Lisa's Lingo (www.thelisaparisi.com), a great blog that describes classroom practice in light of Universal Design for Learning, and Langwitches (www.langwitches.org/blog), an excellent blog that provides concrete examples of technology-infused literacy instruction. See the full listing of blogs in Tool Repository C for more resources like these.

Once I've identified something that I think my students will enjoy, I begin to plan the learning event. I determine the objectives, craft a relevant assessment, and prepare any necessary materials. It's important to note that I do those activities precisely in that order. You must identify the learning objective and relevant assessment *before* determining the learning activities that will assist students in achieving mastery.

If you select activities because they're "fun" or "cool," all of your "user-generated learning" is for naught. Excellent instructional design must bolster all the decisions you make as a learner and classroom teacher. For more information on planning for mastery and writing superior educational objectives, consult Anne Reeves's (2011) book on learning objectives, *Where Great Teaching Begins*.

After the implementation of the lesson, I always jot a few notes to myself in my plan book or on a post-it. Then I wait. I need a little bit of distance from the lesson to ensure that I'm objectively reviewing the entire experience. This delay also gives me time to review any student work or student assessments produced during the lesson, and it helps me determine if the learning activities were successful in helping students achieve the identified learning objectives.

When I'm ready, I pull out my laptop or iPad. And I write. And I write. I typically try to answer the following questions:

- Did the lesson actually work? Did my students meet the objective I set forth? The answer to this fundamental question must always be data-informed and based on student assessments results. If you crafted a good assessment, this is easy to determine. If your assessment is not clear or does not directly relate to your learning objectives, this question becomes vague and difficult to answer.

- Did the lesson support my personal mission statement as an educator? Every year or so, I answer the following question for myself: If I've done my job well, what will my students be able to do when they leave my class? I write down the answer and post it in the front cover of my plan book. When I evaluate the effectiveness of a new lesson, I always refer to that mantra. Did I support my ideas through the lesson, or did I just propagate the status quo? Sometimes, especially when you feel that you've created a particularly engaging learning activity, it is difficult to recognize that the outcomes experienced by the students were subpar or unrelated to what you value as an educator. Remember to stay true to what matters for students.

- What made the lesson successful?

- What could be done to improve the lesson?

- Do I need to provide follow-up instruction or enrichment for any students? For me, the answer to this question is always *yes*. I personally think it's impossible to meet everyone's needs in a single lesson.

Consider a small slice of educational philosophy and determine your position on it. You are an educator. You are a professional. You are an expert. So consider what educational bloggers put forth, and offer your own opinion. The best reflections are a synthesis of informed opinions, personal experience, and research. For example, "the flipped classroom" is a facet of educational philosophy that is becoming increasingly popular. The flipped classroom philosophy states that teachers should provide students with access to lectures or direct instruction for homework via videos or podcasts, allowing class time to be allotted for interactive practice and exploration. (To learn more about the flipped classroom, check out Jon Bergmann and Aaron Sams's blog at http://flipped-learning.com/.)

It's likely that some content about the flipped classroom will show up as you curate. Tag a few articles and craft your own opinion. Is it a good strategy for kids? Why or why not? By answering these questions, you will begin to "own" the information and ideas that you curate.

Use your curated material to craft a personalized goal to improve your instruction and your students' learning. Huh? How does reading articles translate into a goal? Well, if your curation strategies are effective, you should be receiving quite a few examples of best practices instruction in your inbox each day. Is there one particular area that interests you most? Perhaps it's literacy instruction. Let's say you want to find ways to increase student outcomes in literacy.

Check out everything you've curated and set a SMART goal (Doran, 1981). SMART stands for small, measurable, achievable, regular, and timely.

Here's an example for literacy instruction:

All my third-grade students will be reading at a level M according to Fountas and Pinnell by the end of December.

Small: It's a small goal that I can easily identify.

Measurable: Since I track my students' reading levels during guided reading instruction, I am constantly tracking this goal.

Achievable: Level M is considered to be average at this stage of development for third graders, so it's an achievable goal.

Regular: Students get regular reading instruction that I can adjust to meet the goal.

Timely: There is a specific time frame for achieving the goal during which I can track progress.

I could use all of the content that I curated about literacy instruction to beef up my reading instruction to help me meet my SMART goal. Maybe a review of my curated materials would help me find a gap in my instructional practice: my students don't have opportunities for regular fluency practice. I could find a few instructional strategies, such as fluency poems and reader's theater, and I could introduce them into my classroom.

As I moved toward the goal I had identified, it would be necessary to continuously reflect upon my practice and my students' performance. Was it working? What should I change? What should I keep the same?

Most importantly, make sure that the measure you choose to monitor is worthy of your time and attention in the first place. Will a "level M" rating on the Fountas and Pinnell assessment show that your students are able to read and comprehend at a high level? All assessments are NOT created equal, and the assessment that you select can be the critical factor that determines the true success or failure of your initiative.

Methods of Reflection

Okay, so you've settled on the content and format of your reflection. Now, where does it go? It's probably been your experience that reflection is a highly personal process. I'd like to offer you a paradigm shift. Reflection should be as public as possible.

The methods of reflection occur on a continuum based on your needs. You can move along the continuum toward public discourse as your confidence grows. Let's examine the methods of reflection from private to public.

Personal Journal, Word Document, or Audio Recording

Reflection in these formats occurs for your eyes only. While it's important to note that reflection is not synonymous with writing, journaling is the preferred method for many teachers. When your reflection remains this private, you isolate yourself from competing views or helpful ideas. However, since you are the only audience of your reflection, it is easier to take intellectual risks and be critical of your own practice.

Semiprivate Conversations or Meetings

Reflection in these formats typically occurs as part of a protocol. Sometimes termed "critical friends," this type of reflection occurs in the context of a small collegial group (National School Reform Faculty, 2012). Opening up your reflection to a small jury of peers can provide a variety of benefits. First, your colleagues can learn more about you as an educator, thus supporting departmental collaboration. Second, having feedback from your peers allows you to consider alternative viewpoints, content interpretations, lesson experience, and educational strategies. Finally, sharing your reflection in a small group can help you realize that you are not the only educator facing challenges each day.

Public Blog or Online Posting

When considering reflection in a public or an online learning space, it is critical to remember that your words must be reflective about your teaching and your practice, *not* about

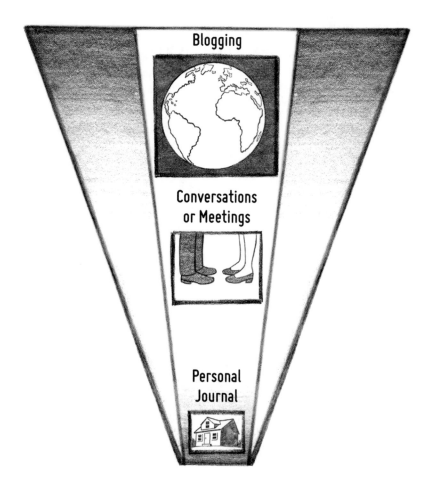

your students. Do not mention students by name or reveal distinguishing characteristics about them. Also, you may wish to leave your organization anonymous. These practices will ensure that thoughts and ideas about your practice do not conflict with the health and safety of your students or your educational organization at large. However, once you find an appropriate voice for your reflections in a public space, the benefits are overwhelming. Visitors will be diverse, and they will offer challenges beyond your immediate experiences. For example, some of the most challenging comments on my blog come from educators in Australia. The opportunity to dialogue with educators across the world certainly helps me make meaning of information that I've curated. Further, if I curate information and come to a conclusion that is misinformed or disproven, the online community is quick to respond. This helps me be thoughtful during the meaning-making process, and it ensures that stopgaps are in place to keep me from getting wildly off track. (I would also consider my voracious reading of educational research as another, more validated, method to ensure this!) Reflection in a public space creates a transparency for learning that benefits education. For more tips on starting your own blog, see Tool Repository E at the end of this book.

Remember Richard?

Well, Richard's reflective blog writing took off. He's now known as the author of *Free Technology for Teachers* at www .freetech4teachers.com. Many teachers count on Richard's amazing resource to identify new tips, tools, and strategies to use in their classrooms. Although many have called him an "ed-tech genius guy" or "the all-knowing tech tool man," he is much more humble about his public approach to learning and reflection. He says, "I am not a genius or any of the other labels that have been assigned to me. I take things and I repurpose them." He says that 70 percent of his information comes through 300 Really Simple Syndication (RSS) feeds (remember Google Reader?) delivered to him each day. Another 20 percent of his information comes from Twitter, and 10 percent comes from blog comments or e-mails.

As many educators trying user-generated learning will tell you, it is not the product but the process that they find most valuable. Richard says, "It's really about the thinking. The act of finding resources and thinking about them changes your practice. The more exploring I do, the more I try, and the more I learn."

Richard uses innovating techniques and his favorite standbys in the classroom each day, but he is simultaneously contributing to the learning of teachers across the nation.

The second phase of user-generated learning requires you to reflect and make meaning out of what you have curated. While this is often regarded as a highly personal, internal process, sharing information at this stage via blogging or other online spaces can encourage deeper understanding due to the existence of vibrant feedback from the educational community. Reflect often, reflect diversely, and reflect publicly.

Your To-Do List

1. **Sign up for Blogger.** Go to www.blogger.com and sign up for a free account. If you've already signed up for Google Reader, you can use the same login information for Blogger. Neat, huh?

2. **Write a post.** Write and post a reflection about a recent lesson you taught to your students. Share the good, the bad, and the ugly!
3. **Share your post.** Use Twitter or e-mail to share a link to your post. Encourage others to leave comments that might prove helpful to you.

Contribution

5

I wondered why somebody didn't do something.
Then I realized, I am somebody.

—Unknown

Meet Kim Sivick

Kim was an elementary school teacher at an independent school in Philadelphia. Many of her students came from affluent backgrounds, and she wanted a way for them to experience the world beyond their front doors. While she had tried videos and books, she really wanted the students to contribute to the global community at large. Kim started by using social networks for personal use, but she quickly saw the power of online tools to connect her school to the world. At first, she started a blog for her class. Students started blogging and sharing about countries they were studying in school. Soon, other people started to notice the students' work. Opportunities for collaboration starting popping up, including a project with American first graders and Australian year two students. Students' contributions were deemed valuable, which was very motivating. Collaboration and learning grew.

The Need for Contribution

Once you have synthesized the materials and information that you've curated, you need to use your new knowledge to give back to the learning community. In essence, your growing understandings would not exist without the network, because there would be nothing to curate!

There is a pronounced need for you to contribute to the learning spaces and people from which you learn. And while you might be asking "What do I have of value?" the answer is simple: you have your experiences, your classroom, and your teaching to share. In essence, your voice is unique and it offers the network a different perspective. Regardless of your level of expertise, the simple act of contribution builds reciprocal learning relationships that prove very powerful.

Ways to Contribute

Free, grassroots ways to distribute learning abound. Once you've created an idea, lesson plan, template, or framework that is worth sharing, you can use a variety of methods to communicate your creations in a public space.

Placing a contribution in a public space can be defined in many different ways. For some people, the public space is defined by using social media online. For others, the public space can be your grade-level team or "critical friends" group. Just as there is a continuum for reflection, there is also a continuum for contribution.

Personally, I contribute to both the online space and the physical space. I not only rely on my virtual networks to amplify the critical understandings of my work but also organize gatherings of local teachers who facilitate learning (more on that later). Your contributions should be highly personalized to reflect your strengths and your newly formed understandings.

It's important to note that your contribution may be an artifact, or you may contribute by serving as the social glue that holds learning together. For example, I run regularly with a group of women. While I'm not the fastest or leanest runner, I'm the "organizer." I make sure that we keep our promises and log some miles each week. Keeping groups together requires relationships. In learning, you can contribute by getting the right people into the right discussion and right spaces.

If you opt to contribute to your learning network online, there are many options. What follows are a few ideas to get you started.

Online Ways to Contribute

If you opt to contribute to your learning network online, there are many options. Here are a few ideas to get you started:

Build an Online Resource

Do you have a highly successful unit? Maybe you created a rubric that really helps students metacognitively reflect upon their performance. Perhaps you summarized leading educational research in a short blog post. In any case, all the curation and reflection that you've done should be evident in the artifacts of your teaching practice.

Here are some examples of teacher-created, noncommercial online resources:

Cybrary Man (www.cybraryman.com/). This site is compiled by a retired New York City teacher librarian, Jerry Blumengarten.

Richard Byrne's Guides (www.freetech4teachers.com/p/free-downloads.html). This site has eight extremely detailed guides about using different technology tools in your classroom. Richard is a high school social studies teacher in Maine.

Free Downloads

Welcome to Free Technology for Teachers!

The eight free guides below will give you a sense of what this blog is all about. Every day Free Technology for Teachers provides teachers with free websites and resources that they can use in their classrooms. Take a look at this post or this post to get a better sense of the type of post you'll find here. If you like what you see, please subscribe to the blog using the RSS or Email subscription options by clicking the icons to the right.

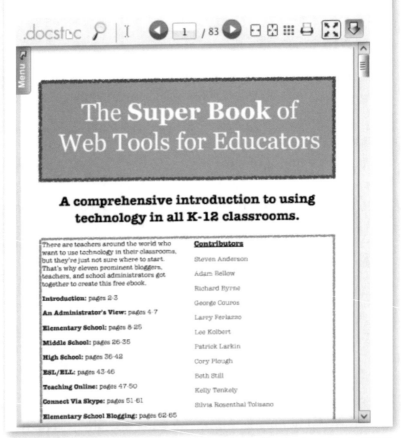

Twitter Handbook for Teachers by Tomaz Lasic (www .scribd.com/doc/14062777/Twitter-Handbook-for -Teachers). Tomaz is a Big Picture Advisory teacher from Australia. He is very active with social media.

Khan Academy (www.khanacademy.org/). Khan Academy is a site full of instructional videos created by Salman Khan. The site originally started as a way for Salman to tutor his niece. Now it has grown (with the help of grant money) and includes thousands of videos.

Winter Wonderland Wiki (http://winterwonderland .wikispaces.com/). The Winter Wonderland Wiki is a winter project that requires diverse collaboration. Classrooms from across the United States work together to solve problems and share ideas.

Join an Online Conversation and Add Value

Every Tuesday at 12 and 7 p.m. EST, there is a hashtag chat called #edchat. A hashtag chat occurs when a group of individuals decide to get together virtually and connect their conversations on a specific topic using a hashtag. (A hashtag is a label that can be used to organize tweets. See "Twitter" under Tool Repository A for more information and examples.) So each week, educators in the Twitter community vote on a relevant topic. Then everyone comes together to discuss the issue, share links, and gather diverse perspectives.

The first time you participate in a hashtag chat, it may seem overwhelming. It is seemingly impossible to follow the endless stream of comments. A good method is to use Tweetchat (http://tweetchat.com) to sign into your Twitter account. This allows you to control when the page refreshes, giving you adequate time to read and respond to the community's comments. It also allows you to view only tweets with a particular

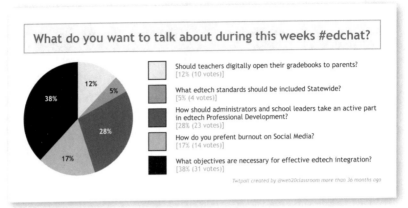

hashtag, helping you to focus on the conversation as it unfolds in real time.

When you participate in a hashtag chat, it is important for you to engage others inside the virtual space. You must go beyond reading and saving relevant links. You must respond to others' ideas, probing their thinking. Retweeting and replying is also encouraged. Interacting in the #edchat space has helped me build connections on Twitter, and it has helped

Reproduced from http://twitter.com.

me personalize my follower list. While I don't participate every week, I do try to engage in #edchat at least a few times each year.

There are also many other chats beyond #edchat, including #elemchat, #ellchat, and #SGAchat. Check cybraryman .com/chats.html for a complete listing of educational chats and when they occur.

Comment on Blogs

Another way to join an online conversation is to comment on educators' blog posts. Blog comments are a vibrant space in the educational community, and there are often fervent debates following blog posts. I recommend Scott McLeod (http:// dangerouslyirrelevant.org/) as an insightful blog author who also cultivates a rich dialogue of blog comments. By contributing to this conversation, you enrich not only the original post but also the blogger's perceptions. When leaving blog comments, remember to be courteous. Consider the following netiquette suggestions:

+ Use your real name or some version of your real name. Your blog comments help you cultivate your digital footprint and they also add accountability to your ideas.

- Be polite. While it is certainly okay to disagree, remember to disagree with dignity. Don't say anything in a blog comment that you wouldn't say in person. The world of educational blogging is relatively small, and someday you may meet these people in professional circles. (I'm serious!)
- Cite and recognize other comments before posting your own. The only thing more annoying than an impolite blog comment is an uninformed one. Make sure you read all the comments before posting. Otherwise you end up with a slew of repetitious, disjointed comments. It is courteous to acknowledge prior blog comments in the stream and recognize other commenters by name (or username).
- Provide evidence, links, and helpful connections when possible. If you have a resource that is related to a blog post, put it directly into the comments. This helps other teachers connect with meaningful information sources.

Respond to Inquiries on Twitter

On Twitter, someone talking to you will use the @ symbol. This is called a reply. Be sure to check your replies somewhat regularly, and respond to any inquiries. For example, I receive a few replies each day asking for app recommendations, information about where I work, or my thoughts on a particular topic. It will take you about three minutes to craft a 140-character response and engage with the Twitter community. Your response not only contributes to the community at large but also helps you to build meaningful relationships in a virtual space.

suludavis: Do we know real innovation when we see it? #Educon

6:46pm, Jan 27 from Twitter for iPhone

sheamusburns: @suludavis you enjoying educon so far? Valuable or Pep Rally?

6:47pm, Jan 27 from Twitter for Mac

suludavis: @sheamusburns excellent conversations so far at #Educon

9:35pm, Jan 28 from Twitter for iPhone

sheamusburns: @suludavis Glad to hear it. Any highlights/speakers I should search out particularly? #educon #edchat #edtech

12:40am, Jan 29 from Twitter for Mac

suludavis: @sheamusburns I was totally jazzed about new approaches to online learning from @kristenswanson, also loved #hackjam at #educon

1:51pm, Jan 29 from Twitter for iPad

sheamusburns: @suludavis @kristenswanson What are these "new approaches to online learning?" would love to hear more! #edtech #educon #edchat

7:58pm, Jan 31 from Twitter for Mac

kristenswanson: @sheamusburns @suludavis You can check out my 5 min preso here: http://t.co/XuyFwhVV Enjoy!

8:09pm, Jan 31 from Twitter for iPhone

sheamusburns: @kristenswanson @suludavis Thanks listening now. These are the questions I've been thinking about! http://t.co/4fHyt7Hl #edtech #edchat

8:16pm, Jan 31 from Twitter for Mac

kristenswanson: @sheamusburns I think the answer to your post is simple: gaming.

4:06pm, Feb 01 from HootSuite

sheamusburns: @kristenswanson yes. headed there myself re: gaming.

4:14pm, Feb 01 from Twitter for Mac

crafty184: I haven't heard a single person mention Google+ here at #educon. I find that interesting.

10:45am, Jan 29 from Osfoora HD

kristenswanson: @crafty184 Agree. It hasn't been a vibrant space for me lately. Or maybe we are moving beyond tools to concepts?

10:48am, Jan 29 from Twitter for iPad

crafty184: @kristenswanson although we sure have been on twitter a lot.

10:58am, Jan 29 from Osfoora HD

kristenswanson: @crafty184 But have we talked about Twitter? Much less so than last year...

11:00am, Jan 29 from Twitter for iPad

crafty184: @kristenswanson fair enough. We sure don't seem to be adopting plus though. Its like twitter is just assumed. Interesting to me.

11:01am, Jan 29 from Osfoora HD

kristenswanson: @crafty184 I do like plus. I just haven't given up anything to include it. I do use handouts pretty often though.

11:50am, Jan 29 from Twitter for iPad

geraldaungst: @kristenswanson @crafty184 Twitter is much simpler than G+. You can also access it more easily. G+ is still a destination.

11:53am, Jan 29 from Seesmic

Be the Social Glue of Your Social Network

As I said earlier, providing a physical or virtual space where people can engage in structured or unstructured learning is another way to contribute.

Organize Your Own #Chat

Perhaps you've participated in #edchat. What's next? Why not organize your own hashtag chat? All you need to do is decide on your topic/hashtag and regular time. Then, get the word out! I think you will be surprised at how many people will engage in your conversation!

Online Global Educational Collaborative
and Other Online Conferences

The Global Education Collaborative hosts an international conference every year online. It calls for presenters who are teachers and experts in the field. You can organize and propose an hour-long session. Then simply deliver and engage using your web browser. Be sure to check out the Global Education site (http://globaleducation.ning.com/page/2011-conference) for more details. Applications to present are usually distributed in the fall.

In addition to the online Global Education Collaborative, there are several other online virtual conferences, such as K12 Online (http://k12onlineconference.org/) and Trends in Library Training and Learning (www.webjunction.org/trends -training-learning). Presenting at one would be a substantial way to contribute.

There are many ways to contribute using the online space. Best of all, sharing your talents in this medium is usually free and requires only your time! Don't let the virtual space

intimidate you; educators I have met have been extremely welcoming and forgiving as I learned!

Formal Events

Hosting a formal event at your school or local university can also provide a significant contribution to teacher learning and exploration. A formal event can range from an intimate meeting of colleagues to a pseudo-educational conference. Consider the following examples or models.

TEDx

Perhaps you've seen TED talks on the web. TED stands for Technology, Entertainment, and Design. If you haven't seen the TED website, stop reading this book *right now* and go visit www.ted.com. The concept of TED is based upon the fact that everyone has at least one good idea to improve the world. People give 18-minute speeches (the time limit is strictly enforced) that are typically archived and stored online for free. You must be invited to attend the annual TED conference in Palm Springs, California, and a ticket will cost you a few thousand dollars. So, while it's a beneficial learning experience, the event is likely to be out of range for most teachers.

However, local communities have started having their own TED events, called TEDx events. These events feature speakers who share a single idea with a call to action. Each speaker is limited to the 18-minute format, and the talks are typically archived on a free YouTube channel. I have attended TEDx NYC and TEDx Philadelphia, and I was even invited to speak at TEDxPhiladelphiaED.

TED events usually feature a significant amount of social media, including tweets and live blogs. More information on organizing your own TEDx event can be found at www.ted.com/tedx.

Edcamp

Personally, my favorite way to contribute to the educational community is to organize an Edcamp. Edcamps are free "unconferences" that encourage collaboration between teachers. Edcamps are organized using the tenets of open space technology (OST). This means that whatever happens is supposed to happen, and the people who are there are the right people (Boule, 2011). There is no formal schedule. On the day of the event, participants develop and offer conversations. This lends a democratic quality to the day that many teachers find attractive.

There have been more than 100 Edcamps across the country in the last few years. While collaborative meetings of teachers cannot be the only ingredient in a teacher's learning diet, they certainly make the professional development menu a bit more interesting. For more information about running an Edcamp, visit the Edcamp Foundation at www.edcampfoundation.org.

Teachmeets

Teachmeet is a professional learning model that is widely utilized in the United Kingdom. You can see a list of upcoming Teachmeets at www.teachmeet.org.uk/. Teachmeets include micropresentations that are seven minutes in length and nanopresentations that are two minutes in length. There are also some time blocks for open sharing in a café-style format. The goal is to give lots of educators an opportunity to share while keeping audience engagement levels high. Jason Bedell (2011), one of the organizers of Teachmeet New Jersey, describes Teachmeets as

> a particular kind of conference that really empowers educators. No money ever changes hands; it is all about educators helping each other to improve for the benefit of their children. Everyone who wants to present is welcome. We believe that all educators have experience that we can learn from. Educators choose topics based on their areas of passion; this gives every session a sense of urgency and importance because all the speakers are discussing topics that they feel can make a profound impact on our children. (n.p.)

Other Camps: Podcamps, Padcamps, Barcamps, and More!

Most formats that end in the word *camp* describe unconferences targeted to a specific community or topic. All of these events collaboratively create the schedule on the day of the event. The events are offered for free or at a minimal cost to participants. Podcamps focus upon digital media, Padcamps explore iPads in the classroom, and Barcamps discuss computer coding and design. Most of these events use social media, such as Twitter, blogs, and Facebook, to attract local attendees. These events usually procure local sponsors for venues, snacks, and more.

One City, One Book

Many towns, cities, and schools have adopted the "one city, one book" model. The program started in Seattle in 1997, and it has been popular ever since. Community organizers select a book and advertise it widely within the community. During a specific time frame, the community holds a variety of activities related to the book's plot, theme, or characters. These types of events have been especially successful in middle schools where high-interest texts are tied to social events. We can certainly translate this model for teachers. Select a book, and then host a series of events to share about practice and synthesize new ideas. Again, leading a collaborative discussion does not have to be a lot of work!

School Community

Using knowledge that you've curated online to enrich your school community is a very common practice for individuals who describe themselves as connoisseurs of user-generated learning. There are a multitude of ways for you to connect with your local colleagues and make positive change.

Professional Learning Communities

Researchers such as DuFour and Eaker (1998) and practitioners such as Ferriter and Graham (2009) speak to the power of professional learning communities. In their recent book *Leaders of Learning*, DuFour and Marzano (2011) remind us that schools are only as good as the people within them. Empowering teachers as professional leaders can change the entire culture of a school. The work of professional learning communities thus adheres to a series of three tenets (DuFour & Marzano, 2011):

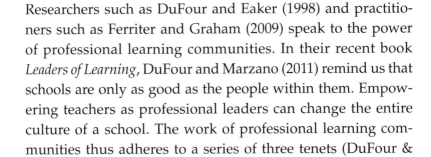

♦ The fundamental purpose of school is for children to achieve at high levels.

♦ If we are to help all students learn, then we must work collaboratively.

♦ Educators must create a results orientation, constantly evaluating and revising their work based on student learning.

When leading a professional learning community, it is best to start with student outcomes that require improvement. What task or performance is especially hard for your students? From there, use research, best practice, and diverse resources to make changes and measure their effect on student learning. If you are interested in bringing this model to your school, I recommend both *Professional Learning Communities at Work,* by DuFour and Eaker, and the blog *All Things PLC* (www.allthingsplc.info/) to help you implement the model with fidelity.

Tuning Protocol

Tuning Protocol is a process through which educators closely examine student work. It was originally developed by the Coalition of Essential Schools to assist the refinement of student assessment systems.

In a Tuning Protocol session, educators bring samples of their students' work and other instructional artifacts. The presenter can offer the group a guiding question to help focus the feedback, both warm and cool. (Warm feedback refers to items that supported goal achievement; cool feedback refers to items that slowed progress towards goals.) The protocol is rigid in nature, and this can make tough conversations with colleagues a little bit easier. The format is summarized on the next page.

1. Introduction (5 minutes): During this time, the group leader introduces the protocol, and members of the group introduce themselves as necessary.
2. Presentation (15 minutes): This time is reserved for the person sharing student work artifacts to provide context for all group members. The person sharing student work artifacts should let participants know what the instructional sequence looked like as well as the makeup of their class.
3. Clarifying questions (5 minutes): Based on the presentation provided by the person sharing student work, other group members can ask clarifying questions to get more information. The questions should not be evaluative. They should be informational in nature.
4. Examination of student work samples (15 minutes): Everyone in the group (except the person who did the presentation of student work) examines the student work samples and discusses them. Although it may be difficult, the person who did the presentation of student work should remain silent during this time.
5. Pause to reflect on warm and cool feedback (2 to 3 minutes): Everyone silently takes a moment to jot down initial reflections on the student work samples.
6. Warm and cool feedback (15 minutes): Group members share warm and cool feedback with the presenter. The presenter is silent at this time, and he or she should take notes.
7. Reflection (5 minutes): During this time the presenter may comment on insights provided through the feedback of the group members.
8. Debrief (5 minutes): Everyone reflects on the protocol experience in general.

The protocol in its entirety is available from the National School Reform Faculty (2012) website at www.nsrfharmony .org/protocol/doc/tuning.pdf.

Faculty Meetings and Professional Development Sessions

Most simply, you can contribute to your learning networks by leading faculty meetings or professional development sessions at your school. Once you employ user-generated learning with confidence, engage your school leadership and let them know that you are ready to contribute!

Remember Kim?

Kim's students took their blogging to the next level. In 2011, she helped her students diversify their knowledge of culture by directly journaling online with a teacher in Uganda (page 80). The work culminated with a third-grade fund-raising project to bring a teacher from Uganda to their school. Although the teacher was unable to get his visa approved for an actual trip, Kim's students used the funds to purchase a computer, webcam, and solar panel so he could continue to work with the students virtually.

Reflecting on the blogging project, Kim said, "I really think that there is a push on technology in education today. But I think for both young students and adult learners, it's about community. That's why people who get involved with Twitter and personal learning networks really like it—because it builds community." Kim's most important belief about education is that learning and teaching are "all about rapport. We need to step back and appreciate each other." You can follow Kim on Twitter at http://twitter.com/ksivick.

Contributing to physical and virtual learning networks is part of the user-generated learning process. Leveraging networks to improve student learning and education at large is a powerful way of contributing. Learning in collaborative networks gives you unique opportunities to explore new ideas and gain critical feedback. By giving back, you only help to make the entire process stronger both for yourself and the community!

Your To-Do List

1. **Participate in an #edchat.** Log onto your computer at 7 p.m. EST on a Tuesday evening and visit http://twitter .com/search. Type in #edchat and hit search. Check out the conversation and discussion. If you use Twitter, sign

into your account and post your thoughts using the #edchat hashtag in your tweet.

2. **Organize a sharing session at your school or organization.** Tell teachers that they don't need to prepare a presentation; they just need to bring an idea or strategy that worked well. Do your best to make the sharing informal. (Bringing baked goods is recommended!)

3. **Attend an Edcamp.** More than 150 Edcamp events have been organized by teachers just like you. Find an Edcamp near your home by checking http://edcamp.wikispaces .com, register (it's free!), and participate in a day of sharing and collaboration. Anyone who attends can be a presenter, so be sure to bring your best ideas! Many teachers have called Edcamp the best professional development they've ever had.

Conclusion

> *Learners of all ages are more motivated when they can see the usefulness of what they are learning and when they can use that information to do something that has an impact on others.*
> —Bransford, Brown, Cocking, Donovan, and Pellegrino

Learning is a journey that is never finished. As you continue to engage in the habits of curation, reflection, and contribution, your expertise will increase. Suddenly, patterns within instruction and student learning will become explicit. You will build meaningful physical and virtual relationships that keep you hungry for continuous improvement.

Our students need us to be our best. Being collaborative, reflective, and informed are a few of the ways that user-generated learning helps us get there. The resources, ideas, and classroom tools that you find through the user-generated learning process will excite your students. Dominic, a third-year teacher from the Bronx, worked with me to use a back channel with his students. (A back channel is another way of describing synchronous posting online.) After two class sessions using the strategy, his kids were begging him to stay after school! (That type of reaction doesn't happen all that often for Dominic.) Those are the types of student changes that effective user-generated learning will bring.

Just as that perfect teacher from across the hall reached out to me, you can reach out to others in both the physical and virtual space. Hone your practice and refine the work of others.

Today's world gives you unfettered access to information unmatched by any other century. The prospects that lie before us pose not only big opportunities but also big challenges. Enjoy, learn, and grow.

Online Resource

I am interested in hearing more about your learning journey! Join the conversation at www.usergeneratedlearning.com for free resources, great conversation, and more!

Tool Repository

Aggregation Tools

These are my favorite content aggregation services. I'm sure that many tech tools will come and go as time passes after this book is published. The world of curation is becoming more and more nuanced each day. However, these tools have been around for some time, and I believe they accomplish the task of aggregation better than any others.

My recommendation is to try one service to aggregate your content. Once you master it, try another. Go at your own pace, and use this section as a reference when you find that your personalized learning needs a change or update.

Twitter (www.twitter.com)

Twitter has been popularized as a free microblogging service through which users can share tidbits of their lives from the mundane to the extraordinary. Most people don't realize that there is a growing legion of educators on Twitter who are using the service to share information, links, and tools. Creating an account on Twitter can help you to collect thousands of tweets without a single click. You can access these tweets from your computer, cell phone, or tablet. If you're not comfortable sharing links yourself on Twitter, that's okay. You can always create an account without a picture and follow users whom you find interesting. (Remember how we talked about "stalking" earlier?) There is no "tweeting requirement" to use this service.

The other thing that Twitter offers is collaborative curation by its users. Many educators use hashtags (the sign that looks like this: #) to add their tweets to a conversation. Remember when we searched #edchat earlier in the book? You can also follow these hashtags to gain access to related resources and ideas. My favorite hashtags are #edchat, #educon, #edcamp, and #edtech. It's important to note that some people use hashtags as the punchline to a quip or joke. Sometimes the hashtag is serious, and other times it's not so serious. Consider the following examples:

Example 1: Serious Hashtag Use

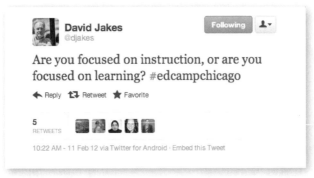

Here, David Jakes is engaging in a conversation at Edcamp Chicago, and he is using the hashtag to add his point to the conversation. I can also add to this dialogue (even though I am not in Chicago) just by using the hashtag #edcampchicago.

Example 2: Not-So-Serious Hashtag Use

Dan Callahan is not contributing to a conversation on "self high fives." Instead, he is using it as a witty punchline to his own personal joke.

If you aren't sure what type of hashtag a user is employing, just click on it. This will reveal all of the tweets linked to the hashtag. If there is no conversation, it's likely a joke.

Getting Started with Twitter

If you are interested in using Twitter as a way to aggregate information, it may not be clear where to start. My recommendation is to create an account and use the following resources to determine whom to follow:

We Follow (http://wefollow.com/twitter/education). This list, which is constantly updated, includes the most widely followed and influential tweeters in education. You can follow folks right from the site.

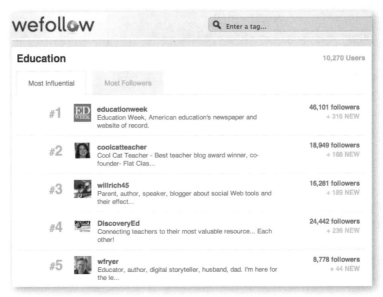

**Twitter 4 Teachers Wiki (http://twitter4teachers.pbworks
.com).** Twitter 4 Teachers is an instructional wiki that has
a variety of resources geared toward educators on Twitter,
and it also has small, individualized lists of twitter users
whom you can choose to follow.

Once you've created your account and determined whom
you will follow, you're done. (You can always follow addi-
tional people at any time.) Log into your account and check
your incoming tweets at your convenience. One nice thing
about Twitter is that you never miss anything. You always
see the most current collection of tweets as soon as you log in.
You simply pick up from the moment you log in, and there is
no backlog of information. While this can make it difficult to
find information from the past, it does reduce the obligation
to check it regularly. Twitter is a great aggregation tool for
beginners.

Google Reader (http://reader.google.com)

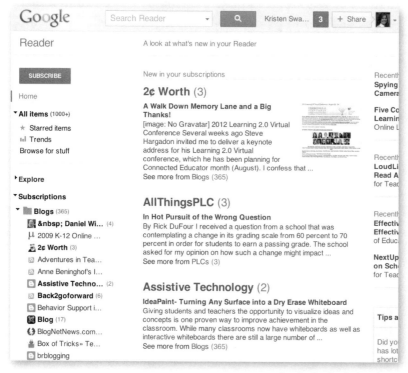

Google Reader is a free Really Simple Syndication (RSS) reader. You can identify feeds (the term *feed* is another way to say blog or website) and enter them in your Google Reader account. You enter the blogs you want (check Tool Repository C for recommended blogs) and Google Reader will automatically update whenever a new piece of content is posted. Imagine it as your "one-stop shop" for content; you can check hundreds of blogs from a single place. Google Reader also allows you to tag and organize all the posts that you read. As an avid Google Reader user, I must note, however, one negative thing that Google Reader can induce: Google Reader guilt. Huh? Guilt? New posts arrive in force all the time. If I've had a busy week and missed my Google Reader for a few days, I can log in to face thousands of posts. It seems so overwhelming that I just want to close the window and forget about it! For me, this service tends to cultivate a feeling of information inadequacy more than any other. To fix this problem, I routinely declare "Google Reader bankruptcy" (aka marking all my posts as read and just starting over) to ease my anxiety! I personally consider Google Reader to be the capstone of my curation process, but remember, curation is a highly individualized process.

Paper.li (www.paper.li)

Paper.li compiles a free "newspaper" from a variety of sources that you select. You can also have the newspaper e-mailed to you daily, weekly, or monthly. It's up to you. You control the volume of the flow of information to meet your needs. One barrier to using Paper.li is that you need to have a Twitter account to use it. Once you've created your Twitter account and followed some interesting educators, Paper.li takes care of itself. Here is an example of my Paper.li newspaper:

Reproduced from www.paper.li.

Flipboard (http://flipboard.com/)

Flipboard is an app that works on mobile devices, such as smart phones and tablets. It is a free application that you can download from the iTunes app store or the Android store. When you open the application, you determine which sources you would like to read. Flipboard provides a variety of educational and popular content from which to choose. You can also plug in your Google Reader and Twitter accounts. (See how impossibly layered your aggregation can be?) Once you've identified your sources, Flipboard creates a personal magazine for you to read. The articles appear in a highly stylized format, and much of the "visual noise" that is identified when using Google Reader or Twitter can be silenced by using this app. One of my favorite things about Flipboard is its portability. You can read your information anywhere on your phone or tablet. It also helps you take advantage of on-the-spot opportunities for learning, and it does not leave you feeling overwhelmed because it picks up with the most recent content only. Flipboard is part of my personal curation process. Since I can mix in news as well as educational blog content, it serves as my daily morning newspaper.

Zite (http://zite.com/)

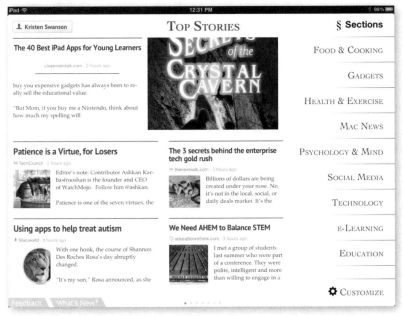

Reproduced from http://zite.com.

Zite is a very similar application to Flipboard. It works on smart phones and tablets, and you can download it from the app store for free. You can connect the app to sources that have already been curated, and you can also include your Google Reader and Twitter feeds. The only difference between Zite and Flipboard is that they offer slightly different news feeds and content sources. Some people love Flipboard and others love Zite. It's truly a matter of taste. However, since Zite is wildly popular as a curation app, I thought it deserved to be mentioned here.

iTunes U (www.apple.com/itunes/download/)

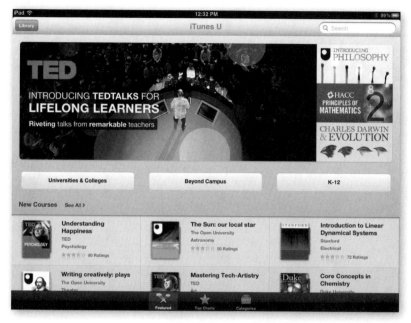

iTunes U is a content aggregation service run by Apple. It can work either inside iTunes (a free program for both Macs and PCs), on an iPhone, or on an iPad. At the time of publication of this book, there were no Android apps for iTunes U. iTunes U posts content from both K–12 institutions and universities. The content can range from podcasts to videos to text. Almost all the materials inside iTunes U are free, except for the textbooks that you can buy to supplement your experience. Stanford, Harvard, and Carnegie Mellon are just a few of the prestigious locales publishing free content. You simply find a course that appeals to your interests, subscribe to it, and the learning can begin! The courses guide you through a variety of modules related to the topic or big idea.

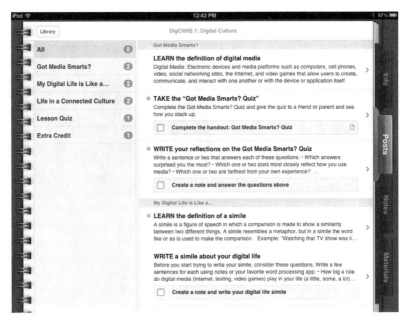

Common Sense Media has an iTunes U channel under the "Beyond Campus" section. It is filled with fantastic courses aimed at helping teens and adults understand appropriate digital behavior. Course titles include "Ending Cyberbullying and Online Cruelty," "Copyrights and Wrongs," and "Managing Your Online Identity." This is a highly valuable resource for both you and your students!

Kristen's Top Ten Twitter Follows

Patrick Larkin (@patricklarkin) is a high school administrator in the Boston area who is very interactive in the social media space.

Meg Wilson (@iPodsibilities) is a creative teacher who is constantly seeking ways to reach today's digital learners.

Karen Blumberg (@specialKRB) teaches at The School at Columbia University. She is a tireless community organizer who educates others.

David Jakes (@djakes) is an extremely accessible and down-to-earth educator who believes in redesigning the educational space.

Marybeth Hertz (@mbteach) is a charter school teacher in Philadelphia who believes that changing education requires proactively changing policy.

Larry Ferlazzo (@larryferlazzo), an ESL teacher in California, tweets endlessly about adapted texts and tools to reach ESL learners.

Kevin Jarrett (@kjarrett) is an elementary school teacher in New Jersey. He is also a teacher leader who enjoys helping others learn inside the digital space.

Dan Callahan (@dancallahan), an elementary school teacher in Boston, is a part of the grassroots professional development movement.

Joe Mazza (@Joe_Mazza) is a principal in the Philadelphia area who uses social media to reach out to parents.

Nicholas Provenzano (@thenerdyteacher) is a playful high school educator who will challenge your beliefs and understandings about the best ways to reach students.

Kristen's Top Ten Educational Blogs to Follow

Free Tech for Teachers (www.freetech4teachers.com). Richard Byrne blogs daily about the best tools to support classroom learning.

The Principal's Posts (http://lynhilt.com/). Lyn Hilt, a principal in Reading, Pennsylvania, shares her thoughts on educational leadership, building change, and instructional technology.

The Tempered Radical (http://teacherleaders.typepad.com/the_tempered_radical/). Bill Ferriter teaches sixth-grade language arts in North Carolina. He often writes posts that challenge the traditional lines of thought on instruction. Comments on this blog are very rich.

Will Richardson (http://willrichardson.com/). Will Richardson is an educator, speaker, and blogger who has been innovating with teaching and learning for more than ten years. Comments on this blog are often fervent!

Granted, but . . . (http://grantwiggins.wordpress.com/). Grant Wiggins, coauthor of *Understanding by Design*, digs deep on issues affecting student learning outcomes. He often references best practices, research, and common sense. This blog is an excellent read.

Langwitches Blog (http://langwitches.org/blog/). Sylvia Tolisano is an elementary school teacher who often shares her classroom experiments that seamlessly integrate authentic assessment, technology, and language arts.

Practical Theory (http://practicaltheory.org/serendipity/). Chris Lehmann, principal of Science Leadership Academy in Philadelphia, shares his insights and struggles as he leads an inquiry-based school.

Lisa's Lingo (www.thelisaparisi.com/). Lisa Parisi is an elementary school teacher on Long Island in New York. Her posts discuss universal design for learning, ways to reach special education learners, and her ruminations about academic learning.

Never Ending Search (http://blog.schoollibraryjournal .com/neverendingsearch). Joyce Valenza is a talented school librarian working in suburban Philadelphia. Her blog explores better ways to teach research in the digital age.

Bridging Differences (http://blogs.edweek.org/edweek/ Bridging-Differences/). This blog is a series of letters between Diane Ravitch and Deborah Meier. Both authors skillfully critique and evaluate educational policy.

Organizing (Tagging) Inside Online Services

Google Reader Tags (http://reader.google.com)

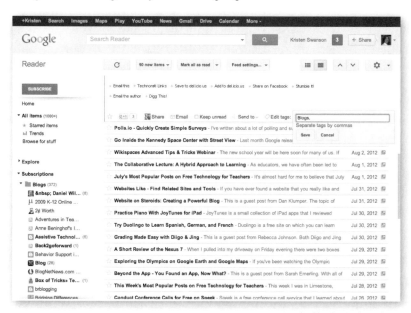

Google Reader is a highly personal tagging experience. When you tag specific items, the tags are visible only to you. Google

Reader prompts you to use tags you've already created so that you don't end up with ten tags about "math." To me, Google Reader tagging is like a personal file cabinet. It's filled with information you've selected, and it's accessible only to you.

Twitter Tags

Reproduced from http://twitter.com.

Tagging items in Twitter is called hashtagging, and it is a highly social experience. Everyone's tags are thrown into the same pot in the Twittersphere. Some tags become very popular and people start adding all kinds of (relevant and irrelevant) content to them. A good example of this is the #edchat hashtag. This tag serves to facilitate meaningful synchronous discussions several times per week, but people also post random items to the tag. For me, tagging on Twitter helps other people find the content I'm saving. However, Twitter tags are not always the easiest way to recall that really great site on the U.S. Constitution that you found six months ago. A hashtag on Twitter is more like sharing than filing.

Posterous Tags (www.posterous.com)

Posterous is a tool that allows many authors to archive and tag items that they've found from other sources (Zite, Flipboard, etc.). You simply set up a free blog and you are assigned an e-mail address. Sending an article to the e-mail address allows you to organize and tag it. You can use tags on this site just as you use tags in Google Reader: as a personal organization scheme. While Posterous does allow for multiple contributors, you are in control of the content and the posts. Again, this is a way to tag, file, and organize content coming from a variety of sources.

The best part about organization in digital spaces is that you can access these resources via the web. That means it does not matter which computer or mobile device you're using; you have all of your stuff on demand. As someone who often presents and shares, I find this a huge bonus. I mean, truly, do you ever know when you'll need to pull up that amazing list of Valentine's Day Games About Phonics? Unfettered access to my online resources has pulled me out of several jams in my life (birthday parties gone awry, long car trips, arguments with my husband over that actor guy, etc., etc., etc.).

Pearltrees (www.pearltrees.com)

Pearltrees is a site that can help you tag and organize from the web. First, go to www.pearltrees.com and sign up for a free account. Then install the bookmarklet on your browser. (Usually you just drag the icon to your browser, and it is automatically installed.) When you find a site you want to keep, you simply click on the "pearl" button on your browser.

Once you've clicked on the "pearl," you can choose which "pearltree" should keep the site. (Think of it as a folder.) All your information is stored in an interactive web for easy reference by you or your students.

Diigo (www.diigo.com)

Diigo is an online bookmarking tool that uses tags. To get started, go to www.diigo.com and sign up for a free account. Then install the bookmarklet. (Just click on TOOLS and drag it to your browser bar.) Once it's installed, you can highlight, bookmark, or share any site you find on the web.

It's a great way to create a curated library of resources for you and your students.

Evernote (www.evernote.com)

This service uses the slogan "Remember everything." It certainly will help you do that. To begin, go to www.evernote .com and sign up for a free account. You can use a bookmarklet, and many iPad apps have the elephant (the symbol for Evernote) built right in! To install the bookmarklet, simply drag the bookmarklet icon (under Tools) to the top of your browser. Once it is installed, you can click on any site you like to save it. You don't even have to leave the site. Evernote allows you to put things in workbooks and give them tags. Evernote collects images, webpages, e-mails, and much more.

Tool Repository

Kristen's Top Five Blogging Tips

1. Get started with a free blogging service such as www .blogger.com or www.wordpress.org.
2. Tell people you are blogging. The more you share your blog posts on Twitter, via e-mail, and through word of mouth, the more visitors you will have. Without visitors (also called "traffic"), your blog will be a very lonely place.
3. Don't get discouraged if every post does not garner a comment. Blog readership develops over time. Be patient. If your content is good, people will find you.
4. Consider inviting several other authors to join you on the blog. This can encourage commenting, increase publicity for the blog, and reduce the amount of writing you have to do to keep the blog fresh and up-to-date. A great example of a highly successful collaborative blog is *Connected Principals* at www.connectedprincipals.com/.
5. Include your blog URL on your Facebook profile, business card, and e-mail signature. This will help people identify you as a member of the blogging community.
6. Take intellectual risks. Honestly, there is nothing worse than a boring blog. Make some interesting choices and invite some discussion!

References

Allen, E., & Seaman, J. (2009). *Learning on demand: Online education in the United States.* Needham, MA: Sloan-C.

Bedell, J. (2011, January 8). *Invite someone to teachmeet nj* [Web log post]. Retrieved from http://jasontbedell.com/invite-someone-to -teachmeet-nj.

Beglau, M., Craig-Hare, J., Foltos, L., Gann, K., James, J., Jobe, H., Knight, J., Smith, B. (2011). *Technology, coaching, and community: Power partners for improved professional development in primary and secondary education* (ISTE White Paper, Special Conference Release). Retrieved from www.iste.org/news/11-06-29/New_White_Paper_New_Standards _for_Technology_Coaching_Debut_at_ISTE_2011.aspx.

Bitter, M. A. (2012, February 6). *Infographic: Study shows the long term impact of teachers* [Web log post]. Retrieved from http://opensource.com/ education/12/1/study-shows-long-term-impact-teachers.

Boule, M. (2011). *Mob rule learning: Camps, unconferences, and trashing the talking head.* New York: Information Today.

Bransford, J. D., Brown, A. L., Cocking, R. R., Donovan, M. S., & Pellegrino, J. W. (2000). *How people learn: Brain, mind, experience, and school.* Washington, DC: National Academies Press.

Carroll, M. W. (2011). Why full open access matters. *PLoS Biol, 9*(11). doi: 10 .1371/journal.pbio.1001210.

Colman, D. (2011, November 18). *Stanford opens seven new online courses for enrollment free* [Web log post]. Retrieved from www.openculture .com/2011/11/seven_new_stanford_courses.html.

Dikkers, S. (2012, March 1). *Where does 21st century teaching begin* [guest web log post]. Retrieved from http://dangerouslyirrelevant.org/ 2012/03/where-does-21st-century-teaching-begin-guest-blog.html.

Dirksen, J. (2011). *Design for how people learn.* New York: New Riders Press.

Doran, G. T. (1981). There's a S.M.A.R.T. way to write management's goals and objectives. *Management Review, 70*(11), 35–36.

DuFour, R., & Eaker, R. (1998). *Professional learning communities at work: Best practices for enhancing student achievement.* New York: Solution Tree.

DuFour, R., & Marzano, R. J. (2011). *Leaders of learning: How district, school, and classroom leaders improve student achievement.* New York: Solution Tree.

Ferriter, W., & Garry, A. (2010). *Teaching the iGeneration: 5 easy ways to introduce essential skills with web 2.0 tools.* New York: Solution Tree.

Ferriter, W., & Graham, P. (2009). *Building a professional learning community at work: A guide to the first year.* New York: Solution Tree.

Flavell, J. H. (1979). Metacognition and cognitive monitoring: A new era of cognitive-developmental inquiry. *American Psychologist, 34,* 906–911.

Fulton, K., Yoon, I., & Lee, C. (2005, August). *Induction into learning communities.* Retrieved from www.nctaf.org/documents/nctaf/NCTAF _Induction_Paper_2005.pdf.

Goday, R. (2011, November 16). *Content curation: Why detecting emerging patterns is crucial* [web log post]. Retrieved from www.darwineco .com/blog/bid/71356/Content-Curation-Why-Detecting-Emerging -Patterns-Is-Crucial.

Harvard Program in General Education. (2012, January). *2012 spring course trailers* [video album]. Retrieved from http://vimeo.com/album/ 1738500.

Heath, C., & Heath, D. (2011). *The myth of the garage.* New York: Random House Digital.

Hopkins, D. (2011, November 21). *A new pln?* [web log post]. Retrieved from www.dontwasteyourtime.co.uk/elearning/a-new-pln/.

Knowles, M., Holton, E., & Swanson, R. (1998). *The adult learner: The definitive classic in adult education and human resource development* (5th ed.). Houston, TX: Gulf.

Lemov, D. (2010). *Teach like a champion: 49 techniques that put students on the path to college.* New York: Jossey-Bass.

Levy, S. (2011). *In the plex: How Google thinks, works, and shapes our lives.* New York: Simon & Schuster.

Marzano, R. J., Pickering, D., & Pollock, J. E. (2004). *Classroom instruction that works.* New York: ASCD.

McClimans, F. (2011, December 9). *12 most disruptive business issues for 2012* [web log post]. Retrieved from http://12most.com/2011/12/09/12 -disruptive-business-issues-2012/?utm_source=rss.

Moore, M. G., & Kearsley, G. (2004). *Distance education: A systems view.* Florence, KY: Wadsworth.

National School Reform Faculty. (2012). *Online protocols.* Retrieved from www.nsrfharmony.org/protocols.html.

Pink, D. (2011). *Drive: The surprising truth about what motivates us.* New York: Riverhead Trade.

Plourde, M. (2012, February 13). *Personal interview* [Kristen Swanson Skype session].

Reeves, A. (2011). *Where great teaching begins.* Alexandria, VA: ASCD.

Rheingold, H. (2009, June 30). *Crap detection 101.* [web log post]. Retrieved from http://blog.sfgate.com/rheingold/2009/06/30/crap-detection -101/.

Shirky, C. (2010). *Cognitive surplus.* New York: Penguin.

Sivick, K. (2012, February 16). *Personal interview* [Kristen Swanson Skype session].

Wiggins, G., & McTighe, J. (2005). *Understanding by design* (2nd ed.). Alexandria, VA: ASCD.